M000036194

West's Law School
Advisory Board

JESSE H. CHOPER
Professor of Law,
University of California, Berkeley

DAVID P. CURRIE
Professor of Law, University of Chicago

YALE KAMISAR
Professor of Law, University of San Diego
Professor of Law, University of Michigan

MARY KAY KANE
Chancellor, Dean and Distinguished Professor of Law,
University of California,
Hastings College of the Law

LARRY D. KRAMER
Dean and Professor of Law, Stanford Law School

WAYNE R. LaFAVE
Professor of Law, University of Illinois

ARTHUR R. MILLER
Professor of Law, Harvard University

GRANT S. NELSON
Professor of Law,
University of California, Los Angeles

JAMES J. WHITE
Professor of Law, University of Michigan

PROSECUTORIAL ETHICS

By

R. Michael Cassidy
Associate Professor
Boston College Law School

AMERICAN CASEBOOK SERIES®

THOMSON

WEST

Mat # 40185093

Thomson/West have created this publication to provide you with accurate and authoritative information concerning the subject matter covered. However, this publication was not necessarily prepared by persons licensed to practice law in a particular jurisdiction. Thomson/West are not engaged in rendering legal or other professional advice, and this publication is not a substitute for the advice of an attorney. If you require legal or other expert advice, you should seek the services of a competent attorney or other professional.

American Casebook Series and West Group are trademarks registered in the U.S. Patent and Trademark Office.

© 2005 Thomson/West
      610 Opperman Drive
      P.O. Box 64526
      St. Paul, MN 55164–0526
      1–800–328–9352

ISBN 0–314–15026–9

TEXT IS PRINTED ON 10% POST CONSUMER RECYCLED PAPER

*I dedicate this book with love to my beautiful wife Mary Beth
and my wonderful sons Seamus and Jack.*

*

Acknowledgments

I owe a debt of gratitude to many colleagues who previously served with me as criminal prosecutors during my nine years of experience in this field. They taught me a substantial amount about what it means to be an ethical prosecutor. Although many of these individuals have long since left government service and moved on to the judiciary or private practice, their devotion and commitment to the public interest continues to inspire me.

Two students deserve particular mention for their thorough and conscientious research and editing assistance. Cortney Merrill and Martha Wilson-Byrne both assisted me at various stages of this project, and performed challenging assignments with dedication and good humor.

I thank my friends and colleagues who teach in the criminal law and professional responsibility fields at Boston College Law School, each of whom has provided me with invaluable insights over the years on topics of prosecutorial ethics. I also thank Dean John Garvey and the Law School Fund at Boston College for the financial support that made this project possible.

Permission has been granted by the American Bar Association to reprint certain materials appearing in Appendices A and B of this work. These documents are available from the Service Center, American Bar Association, 750 North Lake Shore Drive, Chicago Il, 60611-4497, telephone 1-800-285-2221.

*

Introduction

This book is intended to help fill a gap in the typical law school curriculum between traditional survey-style professional responsibility courses and the criminal law clinic. Faculty who teach the standard professional responsibility course seldom have significant time to cover the unique ethical issues which arise for government lawyers in criminal cases. Clinicians supervising student prosecutors typically seek to impart the basic skills of criminal advocacy and some insight into the special role of prosecutors, but often they too do not have the resources to address in detail the special ethical problems faced by prosecutors. I hope that this book can be used both in specialized professional responsibility courses targeted towards the criminal prosecutor, and as a supplement in a criminal clinical course where the faculty member wishes to devote a significant portion of class time to addressing issues of ethics and professionalism.

My personal experience as a prosecutor prior to entering the legal academy suggests that there is an additional need for a book of this sort; that is, as a vehicle for training lawyers employed as prosecutors. Training in the typical prosecutors office—to the extent that there are resources available for any training at all—is typically focused on advocacy skills, local rules of criminal procedure, and office policy. Seldom is any attention paid to the rules of professional responsibility applicable to prosecutors. Regrettably, with respect to issues of ethics young prosecutors are quite frequently left to fend for themselves. Guidance on ethics and professionalism is generally informal, and highly dependant on the young prosecutor forming a mentoring relationship with a conscientious and more experienced lawyer in the same office. Inexperienced prosecutors often encounter professional responsibility "land mines" precisely because they have not been taught to recognize the types of situations that present ethical problems. One of my goals in writing this book is to create a vehicle for training state and federal prosecutors[1] throughout the United States on professionalism. For this reason, I have taken a problem approach to the subject, and I have organized the materials around a set of hypothetical problems typically encountered by persons practicing in the field.

One final word is needed on terminology, specifically the connotation of the term "ethics" in the context of criminal prosecutions. In this book I focus on rules constraining prosecutorial discretion in criminal cases. Some of these constraints come in the form of Rules of Professional Conduct, violation of which can result in bar discipline for the prosecuting attorney. Some of these constraints derive from constitutional protections for the accused, particularly the due process clause and the right to counsel; violations of these constitutional mandates may result in case-based sanctions, including the exclusion of evidence or the reversal of a defendant's conviction. Certain unscrupulous behavior on the part of a prosecutor may violate both constitutional and professional norms, while other behavior may violate one, but not the other. In other words, the two circles of prohibited conduct are overlapping, but not coterminous. At times throughout this book I will are refer to "ethical" violations in a fashion intended to include both unprofessional and unconstitutional abuses of power.

I do not attempt in this book to survey, state by state, the Rules of Professional Conduct applicable to prosecutors. Where I examine professional norms, I will discuss the American Bar Association's Model Rules of Professional Conduct (hereinafter the "Model Rules," select provisions of which are set forth in Appendix A). The Model Rules have been enacted in whole or in part by forty-four states and the District of Columbia.[2] In those jurisdictions, violation of a pertinent rule may result in reprimand, suspension, or disbarment of the prosecuting attorney. At times I will discuss

---

1. With the enactment of the McDade Amendment in 1998, federal prosecutors are now explicitly subject to the attorney discipline rules in the states in which they practice. 28 U.S.C. § 530B.

2. Stephen Gillers and Roy D. Simon, REGULATION OF LAWYERS: STATUTES AND STANDARDS 3 (Aspen 2004).

specific state variations on the Model Rules that shed particular light on a prosecutor's ethical responsibilities.

Of course, not all ethical dilemmas are answered by the
Rules of Professional Conduct. There are many areas of
prosecutorial decisionmaking that are simply not addressed
by the Model Rules, and others that are addressed only in a
cursory fashion that leaves ample room for discretion. Three
other sources of ethical guidance for prosecutors will be
examined throughout this text: the American Bar
Association's "Standards for Criminal Justice: Prosecution
Function (1992)(hereinafter "ABA Criminal Justice
Standards"); the United States Department of Justice,
"Principles of Federal Prosecution" (1993)(hereinafter the
"U.S. Attorney's Manual''); and the National District
Attorneys Association "National Prosecution Standards"
(2nd ed. 1991)(hereinafter "NDAA Standards"). Each of
these three sets of standards of conduct for prosecutors will
be discussed throughout this text, as a supplement to guid-
ance provided by the ABA Model Rules of Professional
Conduct.

The ABA Criminal Justice Standards (Appendix B) were
first developed in 1973 by a commission of expert judges,
defense attorneys, and government lawyers. While these
standards are not "binding" in the sense that violation of
their provisions can result in bar discipline (unless they have
been adopted and incorporated by an individual state as part
of its professional conduct rules) they help to fill some of the
gaps and unanswered questions left by the Model Rules, and
are considered "guidelines that have long been adhered to by
the best prosecutors and best defense advocates."[3] The ABA
Criminal Justice Standards "have functioned in courts and
bar disciplinary agencies much as does a treatise–persuasive-
ly, if that, but not authoritatively."[4]

The National District Attorneys Association Standards
were developed by an association of state and local prosecutors. The NDAA Standards have no force of law, but are used
as a source of training and guidance for state assistant dis-

---

3. *Id.* at 591.

4. Charles W. Wolfram, MODERN
LEGAL ETHICS 60 (1986).

trict attorneys. The U.S. Attorney's Manual (often colloquially referred to by federal prosecutors as the "Bluesheet") is a set of internal, non-binding guidelines for federal prosecutors establishing standards for their conduct in addition to those imposed by law or rules of professional responsibility. Although violation of the U.S Attorney's Manual cannot be grounds for dismissal of a prosecution or reversal of a conviction, a federal prosecutor who violates one of these provisions may be referred to the Office of Professional Responsibility within the Department of Justice for investigation and possible employment-related discipline, including discharge.[5]

---

5. *See* United States v. Pacheco-Ortiz, 889 F.2d 301, 311 (1st Cir. 1989).

Summary of Contents

*

Table of Contents

PROSECUTORIAL ETHICS

*

CHAPTER ONE

WHO IS YOUR CLIENT?

"The qualities of a good prosecutor are as elusive and as impossible to define as those which mark a gentleman.... The citizen's safety lies in the prosecutor who tempers zeal with human kindness, who seeks truth and not victims, who serves the law and not factional purposes, and who approaches his task with humility."[1]

One might be tempted to fault former Attorney General and Supreme Court Justice Robert Jackson for the sexist overtones of this description of the ethical prosecutor, were the statement not made at a time when few women were admitted to law schools in the United States, not to mention the then male-dominated profession of criminal prosecutions. But the major import of this statement remains as true today as it was in 1940. Borrowing Justice Jackson's dated metaphor of the "gentleman" advocate, the criminal justice system demands a level of integrity, judgment, and even-handedness on the part of the prosecutor that it does not expect of other advocates in the legal system. As one expert on prosecutorial ethics has suggested "[C]riminal defense lawyers play close to the line. Prosecutors play in the center of the court."[2] The goal of this chapter is to explore those aspects of a prosecutor's duties that explain this difference in role.

1. Robert H. Jackson, *The Federal Prosecutor,* Speech Delivered at the Second Annual Conference of United States Attorneys, Washington, D.C., April 1, 1940.

2. Bruce A. Green, *Why Should Prosecutors Seek Justice?*, 26 FORDHAM URB. L. J. 607, 617 (1999).

1

Two justifications have traditionally been advanced for holding prosecutors to a different, if not more rigorous, standard of ethical conduct than other advocates.[3] The first justification derives from the prosecutor's role in representing the sovereign. Unlike traditional advocates, a prosecutor does not represent an individual litigant, but rather society at large.[4] As the Supreme Court has recognized, "[the prosecutor] is the representative not of an ordinary party to a controversy, but of a sovereignty whose obligation to govern impartially is as compelling as its obligation to govern at all, and whose interest, therefore, in a criminal prosecution is not that it shall win a case, but that justice shall be done."[5] The office of the prosecutor is a public trust, and the duty to represent the public interest imposes special obligations of fairness and impartiality on the prosecuting attorney.

Unlike a normal advocate, whose job is to provide his or her client with informed advice and then to let the client make the decisions of which options and strategies to pursue, a prosecutor must first make decisions about what is best for society before he can ascertain a course of action to pursue that goal. Because the prosecutor represents the collective "sovereign," he has no personal client to direct his course of action. The prosecutor is forced to make decisions about the course of litigation that in traditional advocacy contexts are entrusted to a client. In this respect, a prosecutor is thus both a principal and agent, whereas the traditional advocate is an agent only. The prosecutor must decide what is best for society, when of course he himself is a member of society. His judgment about societal interests cannot help but be colored by his personal view of the relative seriousness of criminal offenses, his views about particular forms of punishment, and his assessment of competing priorities and resources.

A prosecutor must also appreciate that when he acts as a representative of the sovereign (be it the county, state or federal government) the defendant charged with a crime is

---

3. *See id.* at 625.

4. Attorney General v. Tufts, 239 Mass. 458, 489, 132 N.E. 322 (1921) ("The office [of a prosecutor] is not private property, but is to be held and administered wholly in the interest of the people at large and with an eye single to their welfare.")

5. Berger v. United States, 295 U.S. 78, 88 (1935).

also a member of that sovereign entity. The *defendant* is therefore one of the persons that the prosecutor technically represents. This schizophrenia distinguishes a prosecutor's role from the role of an ordinary civil litigant or the role of a criminal defense lawyer. Unlike other advocates, who have a duty to pursue their clients' interests vigorously within the bounds of the law,[6] the prosecutor has obligations of even handedness precisely because he does not represent an individual but rather the collective good. Procedural and substantive fairness to persons accused of crime is one element of a just society. Therefore, by nature the prosecutor's loyalties are *not* undivided. While society certainly has an interest in crime detection and public safety, society also has an interest in ensuring that all of its members are treated fairly and protected from governmental overreaching. In trying to do what is best for society, the prosecutor must heed society's interest in fairness to the defendant as well as to the victim.

To highlight this contrast, consider the objectives of the prosecutor and criminal defense attorney in a simple armed robbery case where the defense is mistaken identification by the victim. The defense attorney's duty is to pursue his client's lawful objectives, which in most instances means either to avoid conviction or to minimize punishment. A defense attorney will thus have as his primary goal gaining a dismissal of the criminal charges, a suppression of the allegedly suggestive identification, or an acquittal at trial if the former two strategies prove unavailing. Put simply, a "win" for the defense attorney is when his client gets off. The prosecutor, by contrast, cannot assume that his primary responsibility is to secure the defendant's conviction and *maximize* potential punishment. First, the defendant may not be guilty of the offense charged. Because the defendant is one member of the society that the prosecutor "represents," the prosecutor must take the defendant's interests into account in assessing the validity of the prosecution. Second, the prosecutor's obligation is not to convict at all costs, but rather to take steps to ensure an accurate result

---

6. *See* Model Code of Professional Responsibility EC 7–13 (1969); ABA Model Rules of Professional Conduct 3.1, comment 1 ("The advocate has a duty to use legal procedure for the fullest benefit of the client's cause, but also a duty not to abuse legal procedure").

through a fair process; this may mean conducting an independent evaluation of the allegedly suggestive identification procedure before deciding whether to proceed.

Put simply, winning and losing is not a zero sum game for criminal prosecutors, as it may be for some civil litigants. Due to their obligations to represent society as a whole, the prosecutor's obligation is not to "win," but to pursue a just result through a fair process.[7] To that effect, an inscription on the wall of the rotunda in the United States Department of Justice building in Washington, D.C., bears an appropriate admonition for federal prosecutors: "The United States wins its point whenever justice is done its citizens in the courts."[8]

The second reason why a prosecutor has heightened ethical responsibilities derives from the extraordinary power vested in that office. The prosecutor in American society has tremendous discretion to choose which persons to investigate and whom to prosecute. Given the plethora of criminal statutes and offenders, no prosecutor could possibly investigate and prosecute all crimes which are brought to his attention. The most he can hope to do is to create a general deterrent to crime by carefully selecting the defendants and the crimes to pursue. During the investigative stage of a criminal proceeding, the law affords prosecutors substantial discretion to interview witnesses, to immunize accomplices, to conduct physical and electronic surveillance, and to compel the production of evidence before a grand jury that will hear only the government's side of the case. In the area of sentencing the prosecutor also wields substantial discretion, because the decision of what crime to charge or what plea bargain to offer often determines the parameters of the defendant's eventual punishment. Each of these sources of discretion create a tremendous potential for abuse of power. Through the single stroke of a pen in signing an indictment, the prosecutor literally has the capacity to ruin lives and reputations in a fashion that no subsequent acquittal can remedy. In the words of one federal court, "with [this] power comes responsibility, moral if not legal, for its prudent and

---

7. *See* Kenneth Bresler, *"I Never Lost a Trial": When Prosecutors Keep Score of Criminal Convictions*, 9 GEO. J. LEGAL ETHICS 537, 540 (1996).

8. *See* Brady v. Maryland, 373 U.S. 83, 87 (1963) (quoting inscription).

restrained exercise, and responsibility implies knowledge, experience, and sound judgment, not just good faith."[9]

The uniqueness of the prosecutor's role—whether it stems from the awesome power he wields in the criminal justice system, from the distinctive nature of the prosecutor's "client," or from some combination of these two factors—has important consequences for a prosecutor's conduct in investigating and prosecuting criminal cases. The American Bar Association has enacted a specific Rule of Professional Conduct applicable only to prosecutors, detailing some of their special ethical responsibilities.[10] The obligations of Rule 3.8 will be discussed at length throughout this text. Comment [1] to Rule 3.8 is particularly instructive, however, because it describes the prosecutor's role in the following general terms: "A prosecutor has the responsibility of a *minister of justice* and not simply that of an advocate. This responsibility carries with it specific obligations to see that the defendant is accorded procedural justice and that guilt is decided upon the basis of sufficient evidence."[11] A prosecutor's duty to seek "justice" is similarly articulated in the ABA Standards for Criminal Justice.[12]

A prosecutor may not adopt a "win at all costs" approach to his cases. At a minimum, the obligation to seek "justice" implies a duty on the part of prosecutors to take steps to insure 1) that the innocent are not punished; 2) that the process that leads to a determination of guilt is fair; and 3) that similarly situated individuals are treated equally in the criminal justice system. Three essential components of any "just" prosecution are thus truth, procedural fairness, and proportionality.

How does a prosecutor go about assessing what constitutes "justice" in any particular case? While prosecutors do not have a corporeal client they can turn for direction in deciding what objectives to pursue in litigation, they do have several "constituents" in the criminal justice system who have profound stakes in the outcome of the case. Police

---

9. United States v. Van Engel, 15 F.3d 623, 629 (7th Cir. 1993).

10. ABA Model Rule 3.8.

11. *Id.* at Comment 1 (emphasis supplied).

12. *See* ABA Standard for Criminal Justice, Prosecution Function, Standard 3–1.2(c) ("The duty of the prosecutor is to seek justice, not merely to convict.").

officers, victims and court personnel (probation officers, clerks, etc.) are all important constituents of a prosecutor who will attempt to influence his decision about what is a "just" result.

Police officers and other investigative agents work hand in hand with the prosecutor in investigating crime and preparing a case for trial. They typically make an arrest and bring the initial charges against the defendant. Police are also needed by the prosecutor to act as their "eyes and ears" in the community in ferreting out crime. They are very knowledgeable about public safety implications of certain law enforcement decisions, and typically have strong views about what direction the litigation should take. But while the prosecutor must work cooperatively with the police,[13] the arresting or investigating police officer is not the prosecutor's "client," and the prosecutor cannot take direction from them. At times the interests of the police and the prosecutor's assessment of what is in the best interests of justice may diverge.

The tension between police interests and a prosecutor's responsibility to exercise independent judgment on behalf of the sovereign is illustrated by the problem of "release-dismissal" agreements.[14] On occasion, a defendant may be willing to forego civil charges against the police (e.g., for false arrest, excessive force, interference with civil rights, etc.) in exchange for dismissal of the criminal charges against him. For example, this situation may arise when the defendant is charged with assault and battery on a police officer after an altercation preceding an arrest, and the criminal defendant was injured as a result of alleged police

13. The National District Attorneys Association encourages prosecutors to cooperate with the police in providing training to law enforcement officers about their legal obligations, *see* NDAA Standards 20.1 and 40.1, and in developing and implementing appropriate police procedures and forms. *See* NDAA Standard 19.1.

14. A "release-dismissal agreement" must be distinguished from an "accord and satisfaction," which is authorized by statute in many jurisdictions. Pursuant to a typical accord and satisfaction statute, a judge has au-

thority to dismiss certain specified misdemeanor charges pending against a defendant if the victim appears and files a written averment that he has been made whole for his injuries. In a release-dismissal situation, the police officer is not alleging that the defendant has compensated him for any injuries sustained in the altercation; rather, the defendant's promise not to sue the police is the consideration justifying the dismissal of the criminal charges.

brutality. The dangers of enforcing release-dismissal agreements in this type of situation is that it may coerce a defendant to forego valid civil remedies against the police, while at the same time encouraging police to "trump up" criminal charges against a defendant in order to obtain leverage if the police believe that an arrestee might later invoke a civil rights claim against them. In *Newton v. Rumery,*[15] the United States Supreme Court declined to adopt a per se rule invalidating all release-dismissal agreements, but set forth certain factors to which lower courts should look in determining whether prosecutors were exercising "the independence of judgment required by [their] public trust" in deciding to dismiss criminal charges in exchange for the defendant signing a release of civil claims against the police.

Newton involved a civil rights claim filed by a plaintiff in federal court under 42 U.S.C. § 1983 alleging that a town and its police officers had violated the plaintiff's constitutional rights by arresting him, defaming him, and imprisoning him falsely for allegedly intimidating a rape victim in a criminal case. The Federal District Court dismissed the civil lawsuit, because the plaintiff had executed a written release of his civil claims in exchange for the dismissal of a state criminal complaint charging him with witness tampering. The Supreme Court upheld the dismissal of the civil suit, ruling that release-dismissal agreements, which in some cases may "infringe important interests . . . of society," are not per se invalid or coercive.[16] The Court upheld the release-dismissal agreement at issue in *Newton* because 1) the criminal defendant was a sophisticated businessman, was represented by experienced counsel, and had ample opportunity to review the release before signing it; and 2) the prosecutor had legitimate reasons to pursue the release, including sparing a reluctant victim from having to testify at a second criminal proceeding, and sparing the town and its officials the resource costs of defending a civil rights lawsuit. The Court determined that while suppressing evidence of police misconduct is *not* a legitimate factor for the prosecutor to consider in deciding to enter into a release-dismissal agreement, the latter two considerations are consistent with

15.   480 U.S. 386 (1987).
16.   *Id.* at 388.

the prosecutor's duty to protect the public interest.[17] The ABA Standards attempt a similar accommodation of competing interests with respect to release-dismissal agreements, allowing prosecutors to agree to them so long as "the accused has agreed to the dismissal knowingly and intelligently, freely and voluntarily, and where such waiver is approved by the court."[18]

Victims of a crime are other important "constituents" of a prosecutor. Victims are often the primary and most immediate symbol for the prosecutor of society's need for retribution. They have been harmed, and this harm cries out for redress. Victims also are a critical source of evidentiary proof at trial; because the victim of a crime is often the key witness for the prosecution, the prosecutor relies on the victim to prove his case, and the victim's voice in the proceeding will be crucial in seeking the truth and securing a just result. But while the prosecutor should take the victim's needs and wishes into account in deciding what charges to bring and what trial strategy to pursue, the prosecutor does not "represent" the victim, and cannot be guided solely by the victim's wishes. For most crimes there are at least two victims; that is, the actual person or persons directly injured by the defendant's conduct, and the larger society which has been injured by the defendant's failure to comply with community norms. At times the interests of these two distinct sets of "victims" may diverge. For example, even if the primary victim does not need or seek retribution, society may demand it. In these situations, the prosecutor's primary obligation is to pursue societal, not individual, interests. The NDAA Standards reflect the supremacy of societal interests over that of the victim: "The prosecutor should at all times be zealous in the need to protect the rights of individuals, but must place the rights of society in a paramount position in exercising prosecutorial discretion...."[19] While most states have enacted victims rights provisions in their state statutes or constitutions that pro-

---

17. *Id.* at 398–99. The Court also suggested that when a prosecutor contemplates dismissing criminal charges in return for a civil release, "it would be helpful to conclude release dismissal agreements under judicial supervision...to ensure that the agreements did not result from prosecutorial misconduct." *Id.* at 399 n. 10.

18. ABA Criminal Justice Standard 3–3.9(g).

19. NDAA Standard 1.3.

vide victims of crime with certain rights during the criminal process—such as the right to be notified of the scheduling of proceedings, the right to make a victim impact statement at sentencing, the right to the return of seized property at the conclusion of the criminal case, and the right to petition the court for restitution—the objective of these statutes is to give the victim a *voice* in criminal proceedings, while leaving ultimate discretion and control over decisionmaking in the hands of the prosecutor.[20]

Court officials—including clerks, probation officers, and judges—are agents of the sovereign whose interests are sometimes aligned with the prosecutor in terms of ensuring that the criminal justice system runs smoothly, that defendants are treated fairly, and that government resources are utilized wisely. Each of these other state actors may be considered a "constituent" of a prosecutor in the sense that the prosecutor must develop close working relationships with them in order to be successful in their prosecutorial role. These actors may also attempt to influence the prosecutor's decisions. However, the prosecutor cannot treat any of these court officials as a "client" and pursue their objectives exclusively, because each of these constituents represents only one component of society at large. For example, a juvenile probation officer might develop a close relationship with a youthful offender, and may seek to influence the prosecutor to "give the kid a break" if the defendant re-offends. The prosecutor must make an independent judgment about his charging decision and sentencing recommendation based on what is in society's best interests. Although the prosecutor certainly should be guided by the probation officer's feedback with respect to the background, character and personal needs of the defendant, he cannot blindly follow the probation officer's recommendation as if he were a typical client exercising the right to make an autonomous choice about the direction of litigation.

Because the prosecutor represents the sovereign and not a corporeal client, there are very few occasions where a true

20. *See* Walker Matthews, *Proposed Victims' Rights Amendment: Ethical Considerations for the Prudent* *Prosecutor*, 11 Geo. J. Legal Ethics 735, 738–44 (1998).

conflict of interest would prevent the prosecutor from handling a particular criminal matter. A private practitioner, by contrast, must be scrupulous at all times to avoid representing multiple clients with potentially conflicting interests. Nevertheless, there are four occasions where a conflict of interest might arise for a criminal prosecutor. First, a prosecutor must recuse himself from representing the state in any criminal investigation or prosecution where the subject of the investigation or prosecution is a former client who the prosecutor represented when he was in private practice, where the criminal investigation or prosecution involves or is "substantially related" to the subject matter of the former representation.[21] Second, the prosecutor must recuse himself from representing the state in any criminal matter where privileged information known to him as a result of his representation of a former client while in private practice would be pertinent to the investigation or prosecution, unless the former client waives the attorney-client privilege.[22] Third, the prosecutor should not handle a case where the defendant or the victim is related to the prosecutor by blood or marriage.[23] Finally, both the ABA and NDAA Standards suggest that all prosecutors should avoid the appearance of impropriety that would arise where the government lawyer prosecutes a defendant represented by a member of the prosecutor's immediate family—such as a parent, child, sibling, or spouse.[24] The latter situation is discussed in Chapter Seven with regards to a prosecutor's relationship with defense counsel during trial.

21. NDAA Standard 7.3(a). *See also* ABA Model Rule 1.7(a)(2). The practice of "switching sides"—that is, prosecuting a defendant with regards to the very same subject matter on which the prosecutor formerly represented the defendant when in private practice—has also been construed by some courts to offend the Due Process Clause of the Fifth Amendment. *See, e.g.,* United States v. Schell, 775 F.2d 559, 565 (4th Cir. 1985).

22. NDAA Standard 7.3(b); ABA Model Rule 1.7(a)(2). This situation may arise where the prosecutor previously represented the victim, the defendant, or a defense witness in a civil matter while in private practice, and obtained information which could be useful in direct or cross examination of that witness in the criminal case.

23. *See* ABA Model Rule 1.7(a)(2)(lawyer must decline case where there is a "significant risk" that representation of a client will be "materially limited" by the "personal interest of the lawyer.").

24. *See* NDAA Standard 7.3(c); ABA Criminal Justice Standard 3–1.3(g). A similar result is mandated in many states by anti-nepotism rules that govern the conduct of state, county, and municipal employees.

PROBLEMS

1. Defendant Michael Brown allegedly beat his common law wife, Vera Vallace, to the point of near death. Vallace is in the hospital, but is expected to recover. The police have a tape of an emergency "911" call in which the victim telephoned for help and identified her attacker. She was unconscious when the police arrived, and the defendant was found hiding in a bedroom covered with blood. The defendant, who has a past record of violent crime, is arrested and held on high bail awaiting trial on charges of assault and battery with a dangerous weapon.

A few days after the victim is discharged from the hospital, she comes to the prosecutor's office for an interview. ADA Mary Phillips is assigned the case. The victim tells the prosecutor that she loves her husband and wants to drop all charges. The prosecutor suspects that the victim has limited insight into her situation, that she is emotionally, physically, and economically dependent upon Brown, and that she is fearful of retaliation. The prosecutor urges the victim to see a social worker or counselor, but she refuses. The victim tells the prosecutor that if she is subpoenaed to testify, she will refuse, even if it means being jailed for contempt. What should the prosecutor do?

2. Prosecutor Mark Smith is assigned a very circumstantial operating under the influence case ("OUI") in which the defendant, David Page, refused to take a breathalyzer exam. The state's only evidence of intoxication is failure to adhere to marked lanes, an inability to recite the alphabet, and the police officer's detection of an odor of alcohol on the defendant's breath. Smith is called for trial before Judge Hallissey, a jurist who has a reputation for being very tough on the government in OUI cases. Judge Hallissey rarely, if ever, convicts without a breathalyzer exam or evidence of an accident. The defendant has waived his right to a jury trial.

After the arresting officer testifies, the judge calls the prosecutor and defense counsel to the side bar and asks the prosecutor whether he has any breathalyzer or accident evidence in the case. The prosecutor answers "no." The judge says "why don't you rest your case now—we have a very crowded docket today," signaling to the prosecutor that he intends to find the defendant not guilty.

The prosecutor had planned on calling two other witnesses. Should he proceed to put on the rest of his case, or rest? Should it affect his decision that the defendant has two prior arrests for OUI and is considered a major public safety threat? That Judge

Hallissey is the presiding judge in the region, and the prosecutor is required to appear before him on a regular basis?

3. Three young men were arrested for narcotics trafficking following their sale of one kilogram of cocaine to an undercover police officer. All three youths arrived in the same car at the scene of the pre-arranged meeting. One defendant stood on the corner acting as a lookout, the driver stayed in the idling car, and one youth approached the undercover officer and delivered the drugs.

Assistant District Attorney Walter Sullivan is handed the file on the date scheduled for arraignment in District Court. He discovers upon reading the police report and the application for complaint that only the driver of the car and the young man who delivered the drugs were charged with the crime. The officer did not include the "lookout" in his application for a criminal complaint. The prosecutor approaches one of the arresting officers and asks him why the lookout was not charged, even though he was arrested and was mentioned prominently in the police report. The officer informs the prosecutor that the lookout offered to cooperate and provide the police with information about other drug dealers, and that they decided not to charge him in the hopes that he would help them set up future drug transactions.

Given the large quantity of drugs, Sullivan intends to present the case to the grand jury and to have the defendants charged by indictment in Superior Court. Should he honor the police officer's request to omit charges against the third participant in the crime? Is maintaining a good working relationship with the police consistent with a prosecutor's role as a minister of justice? A sufficient reason to forego charges against an otherwise culpable participant?

CHAPTER TWO

THE CHARGING DECISION

The decision of what criminal charges to bring against an accused provides perhaps the best example of the vast discretion held by the prosecutor's office. Many lay persons incorrectly presume that criminal charges are brought by the police. While it is true that the police in certain circumstances have the power to *initiate* the criminal process by making an arrest and applying for a criminal complaint, it is the prosecutor who determines what charges the defendant will ultimately face. The prosecutor may move to amend the original complaint,[1] or in states which utilize the grand jury, the prosecutor may indict the defendant on more serious charges if the initial charge commenced by the police in municipal or district court is deemed to be inadequate. A prosecutor can also move to dismiss a complaint brought by the police where the crime is deemed to be mischarged; in most jurisdictions, the judge has no authority to deny a prosecutor's motion to dismiss unless it is clearly contrary to a manifest public interest.[2] If the prosecutor determines that no charges are warranted, neither a private citizen nor a judge may compel the prosecutor to commence criminal proceedings.[3]

1. *See, e.g.,* Minn. R. Crim. P. 3.04 (2004); Or. Rev. Stat. § 133.069 (2003); Wis. Stat. Ann. § 971.29 (2003).

2. United States v. Gonzalez, 58 F.3d 459, 462 (9th Cir. 1995) ("Separation of powers concerns generally require a district court to defer to the government's decision to seek a dismissal of a criminal charge because a denial of the motion would represent an intrusion upon prosecutorial prerogative."). *See* United States v. Jacobo–Zavala, 241 F.3d 1009, 1013 (8th Cir. 2001); Attorney General v. Tufts, 239 Mass. 458, 537, 132 N.E. 322 (1921).

3. *See* Inmates of Attica v. Rockefeller, 477 F.2d 375, 381 (2d Cir. 1973) (court has no authority in mandamus

The prosecutor's vast power in the charging area is heightened by the reality that legislatures often enact criminal statutes that overlap. The complexity and breadth of criminal codes frequently lead to situations where a defendant's conduct may be construed to violate more than one provision of the criminal laws. A barroom brawl may give rise to charges of assault and battery or disorderly conduct, or both. A bogus tax return may be considered tax evasion, or it may be deemed to be filing a false statement with the government. The Supreme Court has ruled that the due process clause is not violated where two criminal statutes, acting independently of each other, provide for different penalties for the same conduct.[4] Where the prosecutor has the discretion to choose between two or more charges carrying differing penalties, the selection of charge dictates, or at least constrains, the ultimate sentence the defendant will face. The decisions of whether to charge, whom to charge, and what crimes to charge are an awesome source of power for the government lawyer.

In determining whether to charge a particular individual with a crime, the prosecutor must engage in a delicate calculus, having in mind the public's interest in effective law enforcement, the costs and benefits of the prosecution, and the rights of the accused. Among the factors which the prosecutor should consider are 1) the availability and effectiveness of non-criminal dispositions for the conduct at issue; 2) the nature and severity of the offense, and the public safety danger posed by this conduct; 3) the need to deter others from similar behavior; 4) the defendant's criminal history; 5) the recommendations of the victim and law enforcement agents; and 6) the likelihood of conviction.[5]

to order criminal prosecution); United States v. Cox, 342 F.2d 167, 171 (5th Cir. 1965) (court without power to order prosecutor to sign indictment voted on by grand jury). While a victim of crime may choose to sue the defendant civilly, in most states and in federal court the victim is powerless to force a criminal prosecution. However, in one state—West Virginia—victims may petition the court to appoint a private prosecutor where the public prosecutor refuses to go forward with criminal charges. W.Va. Code § 7–7–8 (2004).

4. United States v. Batchelder, 442 U.S. 114, 123 (1979).

5. See NDAA Standard 43.6 (listing "factors to consider" in making charging decision). See generally John Wesley Hall, Jr., PROFESSIONAL RESPONSIBILITY OF THE CRIMINAL LAWYER § 11:12 (2d ed. 1996).

How strong does the government's case against the defendant have to be before a prosecutor may commence criminal charges? It is unethical for a prosecutor to commence or continue criminal proceedings without "probable cause."[6] Probable cause has been defined as reasonably trustworthy information sufficient to warrant a prudent person in believing that the crime at issue was committed by the named defendant.[7] Probable cause is a very low evidentiary threshold, for three reasons.[8] First, it looks at quantity of the government's evidence only, without regard to the possible defenses which may be raised. Second, it does not take into account the relative credibility of witnesses, which is believed to be a matter for the ultimate fact finder. Third, the probable cause standard permits reliance on legally inadmissible evidence such as hearsay or the fruits of unconstitutional searches. For example, if a witness makes a statement to police at the scene of the crime implicating the alleged perpetrator, this hearsay statement to the police can form the basis for probable cause, even if the witness subsequently recants the statement before charges are filed. If the police seize narcotics from the defendant's person or home without a search warrant, possession of those narcotics provides probable cause to support a drug charge against the defendant, even if the search was patently illegal.

The "probable cause" threshold has been criticized as inadequate to meet the prosecutor's overriding obligations as a minister of justice. A criminal prosecution taxes the resources of the courts, detracts time and energy of law enforcement officials from other matters, and exposes the defendant to loss of reputation and to the serious financial

---

6. ABA Model Rule 3.8(a). The Model Rule's use of the term "refrain from prosecuting a charge...not supported by probable cause" suggests that it is incumbent upon the prosecutor to dismiss criminal charges if it becomes apparent to him *after charging* that the charges cannot be supported. *Cf.* ABA Model Code of Professional Responsibility 7–103 (a) (former Model Code provision prohibited prosecutor from "instituting or causing to be instituted" charges not supported by probable cause). A number of state rules explicitly prohibit not only the *initiation* of criminal cases without probable cause, but also the *continued* prosecution of meritless charges. *See, e.g.,* Cal. R. Prof. Conduct 5–110; D.C. R. Prof. Conduct 3.8(b).

7. *See* Gerstein v. Pugh, 420 U.S. 103, 111 (1975); Beck v. Ohio, 379 U.S. 89, 91 (1964).

8. H. Richard Uviller, *The Virtuous Prosecutor in Quest of an Ethical Standard: Guidance from the ABA*, 71 Mich. L. Rev. 1145, 1156 (1973).

costs associated with defending oneself. A prosecutor who commences charges against a defendant based on hearsay or otherwise inadmissible evidence, with full knowledge that he likely will not be able to prove these criminal charges at trial, is not utilizing public resources properly or taking into account interests of fairness to the defendant.[9] Although the probable cause standard has been subject to widespread criticism, it remains the constitutional and ethical minimum in most jurisdictions for determining when the initiation of criminal charges is warranted.[10]

Two other, more stringent tests for what constitutes an "ethical" prosecution have been proposed. The NDAA Standards and the ABA Standards for Criminal Justice suggest that a prosecutor should not commence a criminal prosecution unless the prosecutor expects that it will have sufficient admissible evidence to convict the defendant.[11] The Justice Department manual suggests that federal prosecutors should not charge a defendant unless the prosecutor believes that an unbiased finder of fact will find the defendant guilty beyond a reasonable doubt.[12] Although each of these non-binding standards envision a higher quantum and quality of evidence than mere "probable cause," there are substantial differences between the two.

The "sufficient admissible evidence" standard is essentially the threshold for surviving a motion for required finding of not guilty at the end of the government's case (the criminal equivalent of a "directed verdict"). The pertinent question under this standard is whether, viewing the evidence expected to be admitted in the light most favorable to the government, the state will have sufficient evidence at trial to satisfy each element of the crime charged. To meet this standard, the prosecutor may not rely on inadmissible evidence (e.g., hearsay or illegally seized evidence) because such material will not be admissible at trial. However, like the probable cause standard, the prosecutor need not antici-

---

9. *See* ABA Criminal Justice Standard 3–3.6(c) ("A prosecutor should recommend that the grand jury not indict if he or she believes the evidence presented does not warrant an indictment under governing law.").

10. *See* Carol A. Corrigan, *On Prosecutorial Ethics*, 13 HASTINGS CONST. L. Q. 537, 540 (1986).

11. ABA Criminal Justice Standard 3–3.9(a); NDAA Standard 43.3.

12. U.S. Attorney's Manual, § 9–27.220.

pate the credibility defects of any particular witness, because this credibility determination will be made by the jury as ultimate finder of fact. Moreover, the prosecutor's decision to charge need not be influenced by the strength of any affirmative defenses that he anticipates will be put forth, such as self-defense, entrapment, or insanity.

The "proof beyond a reasonable doubt standard" advocated by the U.S. Attorney's Manual is even more demanding than the directed verdict standard; it requires the prosecutor to anticipate the jury's assessment of credibility, and to charge only those cases where the prosecutor realistically expects to be able to secure a conviction beyond a reasonable doubt after the jury hears from both sides. The difference between the "reasonable doubt" and "sufficient admissible evidence" charging standards is perhaps most starkly illustrated by those cases where it is essentially the victim's word against that of the defendant, with no evidence such as forensic or other proof to corroborate the victim's version of events. In those situations, charging would be considered appropriate under a "sufficient admissible evidence" standard, but perhaps not under a "proof beyond a reasonable doubt standard" if the prosecutor anticipates that the victim's credibility may be severely and justifiably attacked. While the "beyond a reasonable doubt" standard has been criticized because it requires the prosecutor to predict the outcome of credibility determinations to be made by the jury, prosecutors who utilize this benchmark may appropriately be protecting the limited resources of the courts by avoiding costly litigation absent a realistic likelihood of conviction.

Which of these three charging standards a prosecutor chooses to be guided by ("probable cause," "sufficient admissible evidence," or "proof beyond a reasonable doubt") may vary from case to case. There may be exceptional circumstances that warrant charging despite relatively weak evidence (e.g., a serious and imminent public safety danger posed by a defendant with a long record of violent crime, coupled with a need to draw out reluctant or fearful witnesses). There also may be situations where a prosecutor does *not* charge despite relatively strong evidence (e.g., the crime is a low priority for the office, civil remedies are considered adequate, the victim is reluctant to go forward, the complainant has an improper motive, etc.).[13] Perhaps the fairest conclusions that can be drawn from these competing considerations are that 1) a prosecutor absolutely *may not* charge without probable cause; 2) a prosecutor ordinarily *should not* charge without sufficient admissible evidence to convict; and 3) an individual prosecutor may in his discretion *decline to charge,* or may ask a supervisor to transfer the case to another prosecutor, if he personally is not convinced that the defendant is guilty beyond a reasonable doubt. [14]

The low "probable cause" threshold for charging under Model Rule 3.8, when coupled with the reality of frequently overlapping criminal laws, means that prosecutors often have a wide choice of statutes to choose from in structuring criminal charges. Prosecutors thus have the power to charge a defendant with a more serious offense than may be warranted, with the hope or expectation that the defendant will plead guilty to a lesser charge. For example, a killing provoked by a sudden and heated altercation may in some jurisdictions be charged either as a manslaughter or as murder in the second degree. Does the prosecutor act ethically if he chooses the crime carrying the greater penalty, with the intention to allow the defendant to plead guilty to the lower offense if he waives his right to a trial? ABA Model Rule 3.8 does not address the practice of "overcharging" in order to gain leverage. So long as the charge commenced is supported by probable cause, the special ethical rule applicable to prosecutors does not bar the practice of charging for tactical purposes. However, both the ABA Standards[15] and

13. ABA Criminal Justice Standard 3–3.9(b) provides that "the prosecutor is not obligated to present all charges which the evidence might support. The prosecutor may in some circumstances and for good cause consistent with the public interest decline to prosecute, notwithstanding that sufficient evidence may exist which would support a conviction."

14. *See* Uviller, *supra* ch. 2 n.8 at 1156. The ABA Criminal Justice Standards provide that "a prosecutor should not be *compelled* by his or her supervisor to prosecute a case in which he or she has a reasonable doubt about the guilt of the accused." Standard 3–3.9 (c) (emphasis supplied).

15. *See* ABA Criminal Justice Standard 3–3.9(f) ("The prosecutor should not bring or seek charges greater in number or degree than can reasonably be supported with evidence at trial or than are necessary to fairly reflect the gravity of the offense.").

the NDAA standards[16] condemn the practice of "overcharging" solely to gain leverage. A prosecutor looking ahead to the likely disposition of a case must appreciate that a plea bargain sometimes will not be forthcoming. The defendant may insist on asserting his constitutional right to a trial, and may ultimately be convicted of the higher crime which the prosecutor chose to charge for purely tactical reasons. All prosecutors should have confidence that the crime charged fairly and accurately reflects the gravity of the defendant's offense, and be willing to stand by the justness of any conviction resulting from their initial charging decision.

Unlike the decision to charge, there are no ethical constraints whatsoever on the decision to initiate an *investigation* into alleged criminal activity. No threshold of reasonable suspicion or probable cause governs a prosecutor's decision to conduct witness interviews, to engage in non-invasive physical surveillance, or to subpoena persons to appear before the grand jury to testify and/or produce documents.[17] A prosecutor can initiate an investigation into a target at any time, and for any reason, subject only to Fourth Amendment constraints on unreasonable searches and seizures (i.e., physical searches of persons or homes) or statutory constraints on electronic surveillance (i.e., wiretapping telephones).

The currently unchecked authority to commence criminal investigations gives prosecutors the power to "troll for charges"—that is, to investigate a known *person* rather than a known *crime* in order to determine whether the pre-targeted individual has violated any provisions of the criminal laws. This power to troll for charges strikes many citizens as extremely menacing, because criminal laws are so pervasive in our society that all but the most upright and conscientious persons may have violated the law at some point in their lives. Moreover, it is rife with the potential for abuse in the hands of an unscrupulous or vindictive govern-

---

16. *See* NDAA Standard 43.4 ("The prosecutor should not attempt to utilize the charging decision only as a leverage device in obtaining guilty pleas to lesser charges.").

17. A grand jury subpoena is not a seizure which implicates Fourth Amendment protections. *See* Hale v. Henkel, 201 U.S. 43, 64 (1906). The grand jury "can investigate merely on suspicion that the law is being violated, or even just because it wants assurance that it is not." United States v. Morton Salt Co., 338 U.S. 632, 642–643 (1950).

ment attorney. While the Model Rules of Professional Conduct do not attempt to curtail prosecutorial discretion in the area of criminal investigations, the non-binding ABA Standards and the Justice Department Manual address the practice somewhat by suggesting that prosecutors should not commence a criminal investigation based upon their personal feelings about the target[18] or based on the personal or political advantages to be gained by a prosecution.[19]

As noted above, prosecutors enjoy tremendous discretion to select their defendants and to select the charges against any particular defendant. To say that there is any constitutional constraint on "selective prosecution" is therefore a misnomer, because by nature *all* prosecutions are selective. However, the Equal Protection guarantee of the Fifth and Fourteenth Amendments provide citizens with some limited protection from prosecutors who exercise their vast discretion in a discriminatory manner.[20] Generally speaking, a prosecutor may not decide whom to investigate or prosecute based on the race, ethnicity, sex, or religion of the accused, or on any arbitrary classification.[21] This constitutional prohibition of *discriminatory* prosecutions is reflected in both the National District Attorneys Association Standards[22] and the U.S. Attorney's Manual for federal prosecutors.[23]

As a practical matter, however, the Supreme Court has made it exceptionally difficult for a defendant to defeat a criminal prosecution on the grounds of invidious discrimination. To make out a selective prosecution claim, a defendant must show both discriminatory *effect* (that is, that persons of other races, religions or genders were equally subject to

18. U.S. Attorney's Manual § 9–27–260.

19. ABA Criminal Justice Standard 3–3.9(d).

20. Yick Wo v. Hopkins, 118 U.S. 356 (1886). *See* Bolling v. Sharpe, 347 U.S. 497, 500 (1954) (Fifth Amendment incorporates some equal protection guarantees).

21. Oyler v. Boles, 368 U.S. 448, 456 (1962). *See* United States v. Davis, 36 F.3d 1424 (9th Cir. 1994) (recognizing gender as impermissible basis for selective prosecution); Commonwealth v. King, 374 Mass. 5, 372 N.E.2d 196 (1977) (same).

22. NDAA Standards § 42.4 (prosecutor should not consider "factors of the accused legally recognized to be deemed invidious discrimination insofar as those factors are not pertinent to the elements of the crime").

23. U.S. Attorney's Manual § 9–27.260 (in making charging decision, attorney for the government should not be influenced by "the person's race, religion, sex, national origin, or political association, activities, or beliefs").

prosecution but were not charged) and discriminatory *purpose* (that is, the prosecutor made his charging decision on the basis of the defendant's race, sex, or religion).[24] Discriminatory effect is difficult to prove without statistical evidence demonstrating that persons of other races, religions, or sexes committed the same offense over time but were not charged. But the Supreme Court has ruled that a defendant will not be allowed discovery from police or prosecutor's files to make out such a statistical claim unless he can first make a threshold showing of discriminatory treatment.[25] This procedural catch–22 makes claims of selective prosecution extremely difficult to prove.

While the Supreme Court has alluded to a constitutional protection against "arbitrary" charging decisions,[26] this theory of selective prosecution has met with extremely limited success. For example, where prosecutors have exercised their discretion to charge only prostitutes and not their clients,[27] or only bookmakers and not persons who place bets with them (gambling),[28] or only adult bookstores and not adult video stores (obscenity),[29] lower courts have upheld each of these charging strategies against constitutional attack. Courts have accepted a wide variety of less-than-convincing enforcement rationales to rebut claims of arbitrariness— including intentional randomness in case selection,[30] simple laxity in enforcement against others,[31] and a scarcity of resources which prevented the prosecutor from charging all

24. Wayte v. United States, 470 U.S. 598, 608 (1985).

25. United States v. Armstrong, 517 U.S. 456, 468 (1996).

26. *Oyler*, 368 U.S. at 456. *Cf.* United States v. Redondo–Lemos, 955 F.2d 1296, 1299 (9th Cir. 1992) (because courts are ill equipped to review governmental charging decisions, due process protection against "arbitrary and capricious" charging decisions may be a right without a judicial remedy).

27. City of Minneapolis v. Buschette, 307 Minn. 60, 240 N.W.2d 500, 505 (1976); People v. Superior Court (Hartway), 19 Cal.3d 338, 138 Cal. Rptr. 66, 562 P.2d 1315, 1322 (1977).

28. *See* People v. Garner, 72 Cal. App.3d 214, 139 Cal.Rptr. 838, 840 (1977). *Cf.* State v. Baldonado, 79 N.M. 175, 441 P.2d 215 (1968).

29. *See* State v. Holt, 56 Wash.App. 99, 783 P.2d 87, 89 (1989). *Cf.* 227 Book Center, Inc. v. Codd, 381 F.Supp. 1111 (S.D. N.Y. 1974).

30. *See* United States v. Steele, 461 F.2d 1148, 1152 (9th Cir. 1972).

31. Sims v. Cunningham, 203 Va. 347, 124 S.E.2d 221, 226 (1962); Society of Good Neighbors v. Van Antwerp, 324 Mich. 22, 36 N.W.2d 308, 310 (1949).

known offenders.[32] The mere failure to prosecute other perpetrators is not, in and of itself, sufficient to raise a claim of arbitrary or discriminatory enforcement.

A related doctrine of constitutional law which acts as a limited constraint on prosecutorial charging decisions is the doctrine of "vindictiveness." A prosecutor may not charge the defendant with a crime to punish him for the exercise of constitutional or statutory rights. A criminal charge may thus be subject to dismissal under the Due Process Clause of the Fifth and Fourteenth Amendments if it is viewed as impermissible retaliation against the defendant for protected activity. For example, a presumption of vindictiveness will arise where the prosecutor charges the defendant with a more serious offense arising out of the same misconduct after the defendant exercises his right to appeal a conviction.[33] Where a presumption of vindictiveness attaches, the burden shifts to the prosecution to convince the court that reasons independent of the defendant's exercise of a statutory right motivated the prosecutor's discretionary charging decision.[34] Importantly, while the doctrine of vindictive prosecutions has been applied to post-trial exercise of statutory or constitutional rights, it has been severely limited by the Supreme Court in the pre-trial context.[35] Where the prosecutor charges the defendant with a more serious crime after the defendant rejects a plea offer but before the trial itself, the court will not apply a presumption of vindictiveness.[36] The Court declines to apply a presumption of vindictiveness in a pre-trial setting because during the investigatory stage of the proceeding it is more likely that the prosecutor may discover additional evidence that warrants an increased charge.[37] And, because the court has recognized plea bargaining as a legitimate part of the "give and take" of the

32. *See* United States v. Saade, 652 F.2d 1126, 1136 (1st Cir. 1981).

33. Blackledge v. Perry, 417 U.S. 21, 27–28 (1974).

34. *See* North Carolina v. Pearce, 395 U.S. 711, 726 (1969) (presumption of judicial vindictiveness can be rebutted where court articulates independent reasons for imposing higher sentence on defendant after appeal, reversal, and retrial).

35. *See* United States v. Goodwin, 457 U.S. 368 (1982).

36. Bordenkircher v. Hayes, 434 U.S. 357 (1978).

37. *See* Angela J. Davis, *The American Prosecutor: Independence, Power, and the Threat of Tyranny*, 86 IOWA L. REV. 393, 436 (2001).

adversarial system,[38] it has been unwilling to curtail the practice of "upping the ante" with more serious charges where the defendant declines to plead guilty and insists on his constitutional right to a jury trial.[39]

Another form of allegedly "vindictive" prosecution is where the prosecutor brings a charge against a defendant to punish him for the exercise of his right to free speech, or his membership in certain political associations. These cases may be considered a hybrid of vindictive prosecution cases and selective enforcement cases, because first amendment rights of speech and association are protected activities that trigger strict scrutiny and limit invidious classification. Where a defendant alleges that the prosecutor has charged him in retaliation for his political views, he bears the burden of proving 1) that he was engaged in protected speech or activity; and 2) that the state's conduct was motivated in part by a purpose to retaliate or deter that protected conduct. If defendant can prove both of these elements, the burden shifts to the prosecution to prove that he would have reached the same charging decision even had the protected activity not been considered.[40]

As can be seen from these narrow constitutional limitations, a presumption of legality attaches to a prosecutor's charging decisions. Courts will presume that the prosecutor has acted in good faith and in accordance with his public trust, in the absence of strong evidence to the contrary. This judicial deference afforded to a prosecutor's charging decisions is based on several considerations. First, judges are ill-suited to second guess a prosecutor's charging decisions, because they entail a host of public policy considerations (e.g., competing law enforcement priorities, public safety

38. *Id.* at 413.

39. Where a prosecutor increases the charges against the defendant after the defendant files certain pre-trial motions, such as a motion to suppress, a motion for speedy trial, or a motion for change of venue, some courts have also been willing to entertain a presumption of vindictiveness. *See* United States v. DeMarco, 550 F.2d 1224, 1227 (9th Cir. 1977); United States v. Groves, 571 F.2d 450, 454 (9th Cir. 1978).

40. United States v. Crowthers, 456 F.2d 1074, 1078 (4th Cir. 1972) (disorderly conduct prosecution brought against Vietnam War protesters who organized "Mass of Peace" in front of Pentagon). *See* Pizzolato v. Perez, 524 F.Supp. 914, 922 (E.D. La. 1981) (voter fraud prosecution brought against district attorney's political opponent); State v. Parrish, 567 So.2d 461, 464 (Fla. Dist. Ct. App. 1990) (tax prosecution brought against political opponent).

demands, perceived deterrence value of the prosecution) that are considered to be in the traditional province of the executive rather than the judicial branch of government.[41] Moreover, judicial review of charging decisions would impose enormous administrative costs on the criminal justice system—including delays in proceeding to trial, and the reduced deterrence value of prosecutions that may result where the government's confidential enforcement policy is exposed.[42] For each of these reasons, so long as the prosecutor acts with the minimum quantum of proof necessary to satisfy the low "probable cause" threshold, a prosecutor's decision to commence criminal proceedings by indictment or complaint is virtually unreviewable.

PROBLEMS

1.   The police receive a 911 call reporting a domestic disturbance in a multi-unit apartment building in an inner city neighborhood. Neighbors heard occupants of the building arguing and screaming, and other loud noises inside the apartment. When the police arrive they encounter an unmarried couple in partial stages of undress. They separate the couple and interview them in different rooms of the apartment. The woman alleges that the man raped her after she broke up with him and told him to get out of the apartment. The man claims that the two had consensual sex, but that the woman thereafter became enraged after he refused to give her any more money to purchase cocaine to support her drug habit. According to the man, the woman started screaming uncontrollably and throwing furniture, and threatened to have the man "locked up" if he did not give her $200. The police discover a residue of cocaine and drug paraphernalia on the living room coffee table. The apartment is rented by the alleged victim.

The police arrest the man on charges of forcible rape, and take the woman to the hospital for a rape trauma exam. The treating physician at the hospital discovers signs of vaginal penetration, but no evidence of physical trauma. A blood test reveals that the alleged victim had ingested cocaine within the past 10 hours.

Assistant District Attorney Kevan Cunningham is assigned to prosecute the boyfriend on charges of rape. A criminal complaint

41.   *Wayte*, 470 U.S. at 607.

42.   *Id.* at 607–08.

has issued in district court based on the application of the police. Is the prosecutor obliged to go forward with these charges? How should he proceed if he is not personally convinced of the defendant's guilt?

2. Prosecutor Andrew Lawlor is assigned to prosecute a defendant arrested for larceny of a motor vehicle, a felony punishable by up to five years in prison. The defendant has previously been convicted in the same jurisdiction on separate dates of grand larceny and distribution of cocaine, both also felonies. The state legislature has enacted a "habitual offender" statute which provides that any person convicted of a felony who has previously been convicted of two or more felonies shall be punished by a mandatory term of life in prison. Should the prosecutor seek charges against the defendant for simple larceny of a motor vehicle, or instead commence charges under the habitual offender statute? What factors should the prosecutor take into account in making this determination?

3. Assistant District Attorney Sydney Hanlon is investigating a local public official for receipt of bribes and gratuities relating to his official position. The prosecutor has credibility problems with some of her major witnesses, and a statute of limitations problem with at least one of a number of free trips the politician received from corporate constituents. For a number of legal and evidentiary reasons, she decides to charge the defendant with tax crimes rather than substantive corruption offenses. The prosecutor decides to charge the defendant with tax evasion and filing of false tax returns for each of the relevant tax years in which the defendant received corrupt gifts but did not report them as income on his tax return.

Defendant's wife was a joint signatory on all of the tax returns, and accompanied her husband on all of the junkets paid for by constituents. Should the prosecutor charge the wife with tax crimes as well? Is it permissible for the prosecutor to tell the defense counsel prior to indictment that if defendant pleads guilty to the tax charges, she will forego charges against the wife? Is it permissible for the prosecutor to tell defense counsel after indictment that if the defendant pleads guilty to the tax charges, she will forego any further investigation and/or charging into the corruption allegations?

CHAPTER THREE

THE PROSECUTOR AND THE GRAND JURY

In federal court, the defendant has a right to be indicted for all "capital, or otherwise infamous" crimes.[1] The Supreme Court has ruled that this constitutional right to a grand jury indictment is not so inimical to the concept of ordered liberty that the Due Process Clause of the Fourteenth Amendment requires grand juries to be convened at the state level.[2] Over half of the states have abolished the grand jury in favor of other methods of charging and case screening, such as the filing of criminal informations, and the holding of probable cause hearings conducted by judges or magistrates.[3]

In those jurisdictions where it is still utilized, the grand jury is a mechanism both for investigating crimes and for deciding what charges to bring against a defendant. In federal practice and in most states, the grand jury is comprised of twenty-three lay citizens.[4] After being impaneled by the district's presiding judge and being instructed on their general responsibilities, the grand jury acts under the guidance and supervision of the prosecutor. The prosecutor is responsible for issuing subpoenas on the grand jury's behalf to compel the attendance of witnesses and the production of documents, for making an opening statement to the grand

1. Constitution of the United States, Amendment V. The Supreme Court has defined an "infamous" crime as one involving punishment by hard labor or a potential term of imprisonment in a penitentiary. Mackin v. United States, 117 U.S. 348, 352 (1886).

2. Hurtado v. California, 110 U.S. 516, 533 (1884).

3. Andrew D. Leipold, *Why Grand Juries Do Not (And Cannot) Protect the Accused*, 80 CORNELL L. REV. 260, 314 (1995).

4. *Id.* at 265.

jury describing the case that they are about to hear, for examining witnesses, for drafting proposed indictments for the grand jury's consideration, and for instructing the grand jury on the legal elements of pertinent crimes.[5] In a small number of states, the prosecutor may even stay in the room while the grand jury deliberates about a case, in order to assist the grand jury in the event they have legal questions.[6]

The grand jury's work happens in secret—outside of the presence of the presiding judge, and beyond the scrutiny of either the defendant's attorney or the public. Counsel for the defendant plays no role in the grand jury inquiry, and is not even allowed to be physically present inside the grand jury room. Defense counsel is not allowed to cross examine the government's witnesses before the grand jury, to call witnesses on his own behalf, or to make a closing argument summarizing evidence and urging the grand jury not to indict his client.[7] While some states allow an attorney to be present in the grand jury room during his client's testimony should the client be called as a witness, even in these jurisdictions counsel may not object to the prosecutor's questions or speak on the record during the grand jury proceedings.[8]

The grand jury may issue an indictment if a majority of its members find probable cause to believe that the defendant has committed the crime in question.[9] The rules of

---

5. *See* Peter J. Henning, *Prosecutorial Misconduct in Grand Jury Investigations*, 51 S.C. L. Rev. 1, 4 (1999).

6. *See, e.g.,* Mass. R. Crim. P. 5(g). *Cf.* Fed R. Crim. P. 6(d)(2) (federal prosecutor may not remain in grand jury room during deliberations).

7. *See* United States v. Fritz, 852 F.2d 1175, 1178 (9th Cir. 1988); United States v. Scully, 225 F.2d 113, 116 (2d Cir. 1955).

8. In federal court counsel for a witness must stand outside the grand jury room, and his client must request a break in the proceedings to consult with the attorney. *See* United States v. Mandujano, 425 U.S. 564, 581 (1976). Some states allow counsel for a witness to stand by the witness's side inside the grand jury room during questioning. *See* Mass. R. Crim. P. 5(c)

(allowing counsel for grand jury witnesses to be present during examination); N.Y. Crim. Proc. Laws § 190.52 (same).

9. Melvin P. Antel, *The Modern Grand Journal, Benighted Supergovernment*, 51 A.B.A. J. 153, 154 (1965). Although the United States Supreme Court has precluded federal courts from reviewing the sufficiency of evidence before a grand jury in ruling on a motion to dismiss an indictment, *see* Costello v. United States, 350 U.S. 359, 363 (1956), the Hyde Amendment allows federal courts to award attorneys fees to a criminal defendant who ultimately prevails on the charges against him, where the defendant can demonstrate that the prosecution was "vexatious, frivolous, or in bad faith." Pub. L. No. 105–119 [11 Stat. 2440](1997),

evidence do not apply to grand jury proceedings, except those pertaining to testimonial privileges.[10] Hearsay evidence is admissible,[11] as is evidence seized pursuant to an unconstitutional search and seizure.[12] And because the Supreme Court has ruled that a grand jury subpoena does not involve a "seizure" for constitutional purposes, grand jury subpoenas may not be challenged on the grounds that they are baseless (that is, not supported by reasonable suspicion of criminal activity).[13]

Unlike a criminal trial, where the presence of the judge and the ability of the defendant to interpose timely objections may act as a counterweight to prosecutorial overreaching, the power of the prosecutor before the grand jury is largely unchecked by judge or opposing counsel. Because the prosecutor wields such immense power before the grand jury, a grave possibility exists for prosecutors to manipulate these proceedings without detection. The consequences to a defendant from a prosecutor's unethical behavior before the grand jury are great, because an indictment may both sap a defendant's resources and tarnish his reputation in a way that no subsequent acquittal can possibly rectify. Fairness to the putative defendant and respect for the criminal justice system mandate that prosecutors—as officers of the court with an obligation to "seek justice"—resist the temptation to cut corners in grand jury practice.

Professional conduct rules in effect in most states are largely silent about a prosecutor's ethical responsibilities before the grand jury. However, two overarching principles can be gleaned from pertinent case law and prevailing professional norms. First, a prosecutor should at all times seek

reprinted I 18 U.S.C. § 3006A (statutory note).

10.   United States v. Calandra, 414 U.S. 338, 349 (1974).

11.   Costello v. United States, 350 U.S. 359, 363 (1956).

12.   *Calandra*, 414 U.S. at 354. *Cf.* U.S. Attorney's Manual § 9–11.231 (prosecutor should not present to the grand jury evidence which the prosecutor knows was obtained as a direct result of violation of the constitutional rights of the person being investigated).

13.   United States v. Dionisio, 410 U.S. 1, 9 (1973). A target or witness who wishes to quash a grand jury subpoena under the stringent standards of Fed. R. Crim. P. 17(c) must show that there is *"no reasonable possibility* that the [material sought] will produce information relevant to the general subject of the grand jury's investigation." United States v. R. Enterprises, Inc., 498 U.S. 292, 301 (1991) (emphasis supplied).

to preserve the independence of the grand jury as a deliberative body. Second, the prosecutor must take adequate steps to preserve the secrecy of grand jury proceedings.

A. Abuse of Hearsay Evidence

As discussed above, hearsay evidence is admissible in the grand jury.[14] However, many commentators have condemned the increasingly common practice by prosecutors of presenting the government's case in the grand jury via a witness with no direct knowledge of the events at issue (i.e. a witness other than the arresting officer or victim). By calling a witness to testify about observations made by others (whether they are a civilian witness or another police officer) the prosecutor undermines discovery to the accused, and insulates future trial witnesses from impeachment with prior inconsistent statements. While sometimes it is necessary to introduce hearsay in the grand jury—out of respect for the convenience of witnesses or in order to expedite the presentation—the frequency with which prosecutors rely on hearsay to establish probable cause in the grand jury suggests that tactical considerations are also at play in these decisions. A small number of states have enacted legislation to address the problem of hearsay presentations in the grand jury.[15]

Even in the vast majority of jurisdictions where hearsay is admissible, there is a emerging body of authority that suggests that it is improper for a prosecutor to present hearsay testimony to the grand jury in the guise of direct evidence, where the effect of the presentation is to mislead the grand jury about the nature or source of the evidence they are hearing. For example, if a police officer observes a narcotics transaction, he may certainly testify about his observations before the grand jury. If the police officer did not observe the narcotics transaction, but learned about it from a conversation with a fellow police officer who did have direct knowledge of the incident, the first officer may testify

14. *Costello,* 350 U.S. at 363.

15. *See, e.g.,* N.M. Stat. Ann. § 31–6–11 (2003) (precluding judicial review of evidence presented to grand jury absent showing of prosecutorial bad faith); N.Y. Crim. Proc. Law § 190.30 (2004) (providing that rules of evidence applicable to trials apply to grand jury proceedings, but making exceptions for certain public reports and videotapes of child witnesses).

before the grand jury as to what his fellow officer told him. But if the prosecutor calls the first officer to the witness stand in the grand jury and asks him to recount "what was observed" during the alleged narcotics transaction, without revealing the hearsay nature of the information, at least one Federal Circuit Court of Appeals has ruled that the independence of the grand jury has been impermissibly compromised, and the indictment should be dismissed for prosecutorial error.[16]

Whenever a prosecutor relies on hearsay evidence before the grand jury, he should take pains to have the witness explain to the grand jury the basis for his testimony; that is, that the witness is reading from the police report of another officer, is relating information that was derived from an interview with a civilian witness, or is summarizing investigative conclusions reached by other persons involved in the case.[17] This practice is consistent with ABA Criminal Justice Standard 3–3.6(f), which admonishes that "A prosecutor in presenting a case to a grand jury should not intentionally interfere with the independence of the grand jury...." A prosecutor who submits hearsay evidence to the grand jury under the guise of direct evidence is indirectly depriving the grand jury of their right to demand to examine the eyewitness directly, as they could if they had been apprised of the

16. United States v. Estepa, 471 F.2d 1132, 1137 (2d Cir. 1972) (conviction reversed where the testimony of a police officer recounting observations made by others implied to the grand jury that he was an actual eyewitness to the crime. According to the court, hearsay presentations will be countenanced so long as the prosecutor "does not deceive grand jurors as to the 'shoddy merchandise they are getting.'"), *citing* United States v. Payton, 363 F.2d 996, 1000 (2d Cir. 1966). *See also* United States v. Samango, 607 F.2d 877, 882 (9th Cir. 1979). The holding in *Estepa* has not been widely embraced by other federal courts, *see* Sara Sun Beale *et al.*, GRAND JURY LAW & PRACTICE § 9:6 at 9–29, 9–30 (Thomson West 2002), and may have been called into question by the Supreme Court's decision in United States v. Williams, discussed *infra*, wherein the

Supreme Court ruled that a federal court has no authority to regulate a prosecutor's conduct before the grand jury under its general superintendence powers, except in those situations where a specific statute, court rule, or constitutional provision has been violated. 504 U.S. 36, 48 (1992). *But see* Bank of Nova Scotia v. United States, 487 U.S. 250, 261 (1988) (suggesting that an indictment may be dismissed where prosecutor presents evidence to the grand jury that he knows to be "false or misleading," provided the court finds that this deception may have substantially influenced the grand jury's decision to indict).

17. *See* People v. Creque, 72 Ill.2d 515, 22 Ill.Dec. 403, 382 N.E.2d 793, 797 (1978) (no misleading presentation found where it was clear that investigator was summarizing interviews with others).

hearsay nature of the presentation but were left unsatisfied with the prosecutor's indirect manner of proof.

B.   Fifth Amendment Rights of Witnesses

A witness subpoenaed to the grand jury has a Fifth Amendment right to refuse to answer any questions that may reasonably tend to implicate him in criminal activity.[18] Where a prosecutor knows in advance of the scheduled testimony that the witness will in good faith invoke his Fifth Amendment rights and refuse to answer questions put to him beyond biographical data, the prosecutor should not put the witness before the grand jury *solely* to have him assert his right against self incrimination.[19] As the comments to ABA Criminal Justice Standard 3–3.6(e) explain, "[s]uch a tactic is unfair in that the very exercise of the privilege may prejudice the witness in the eyes of the grand jury." A prosecutor may call a witness to the grand jury who he knows intends to invoke his Fifth Amendment privilege only if the prosecutor seeks to create a record to later challenge the assertion of the privilege in court, or needs the transcript to seek a judicial grant of immunity.

While a witness testifying before the grand jury enjoys the protections of the Fifth Amendment privilege against self-incrimination, the Constitution does not require that the witness be *notified* of this protection.[20] Because a grand jury witness is not in "custody," the prophylactic protections of

18. *See* Counselman v. Hitchcock, 142 U.S. 547, 562 (1892).

19. ABA Criminal Justice Standard 3–3.6(e). The United States Attorney's Manual is not as definitive on this subject as the ABA Standards, suggesting that *"ordinarily* a witness should be excused from testifying" if his counsel has indicated in writing in advance of the scheduled appearance his intention to invoke his Fifth Amendment rights. U.S. Attorney's Manual § 9–11.154 (emphasis supplied). The U.S. Attorney's Manual suggests that a federal prosecutor may insist on the actual appearance of the witness if the subject matter of the testimony is extremely important, it is unavailable from other sources, and the prosecutor questions the likely applicability of the right against self incrimination. In rejecting an outright prohibition of the practice of commanding the appearance of witness who intends to invoke, the Justice Department recognizes that "once compelled to appear, the witness may be willing and able to answer some or all of the grand jury's questions without incriminating himself or herself." *Id. See also* Bank of Nova Scotia v. United States, 487 U.S. 250, 259 (1988) (prosecutor not required to take witness at his word for the fact that he intended to assert Fifth Amendment before the grand jury).

20. United States v. Mandujano, 425 U.S. 564, 582 (1976).

Miranda v. Arizona[21] do not apply to these proceedings—even if the witness is a target of the grand jury's investigation and the prosecutor anticipates seeking an indictment against him, the prosecutor is not required to notify the witness of his right to remain silent.[22] The Supreme Court has ruled that grand jury witnesses are not constitutionally entitled to "target warnings" notifying them of their potential indictment and their privilege against self-incrimination.[23] The failure of a witness to appreciate his or her right to decline to answer questions will not require the later suppression of any inculpatory information they reveal to the grand jury.[24]

Notwithstanding this "lack of a clear constitutional imperative,"[25] both the ABA Criminal Justice Standards and the U.S. Attorney's Manual suggest that a prosecutor, when dealing with a grand jury witness who faces criminal exposure, should inform the witness of his potential target status and his right to obtain counsel. ABA Criminal Justice Standard 3–3.6(d) provides that "If the prosecutor believes that a witness is a potential defendant, the prosecutor should not seek to compel the witness's testimony before the grand jury without informing the witness that he or she may be charged and that the witness should seek independent legal advice concerning his or her rights." The United States Attorney's Manual is even more protective of grand jury witnesses, suggesting that whenever a witness is either a potential "target" or "subject" of the grand jury's investigation, the witness should be informed on the record before the grand jury, at the outset of his testimony, of 1) the subject matter of the grand jury's investigation; 2) the witness's right to refuse to answer any questions that may have a tendency to incriminate him; 3) the fact that the government may use any statements the witness provides against the witness at any subsequent legal proceeding; and 4) that the witness has a right to obtain and consult counsel if so desires.[26] Some states have adopted rules requiring

21. 384 U.S. 436 (1966).

22. *Mandujano*, 425 U.S. at 578.

23. United States v. Washington, 431 U.S. 181, 189 (1977).

24. United States v. Wong, 431 U.S. 174, 177–79 (1977).

25. U.S. Attorney's Manual § 9–11.151.

26. *Id*. A "target" is defined in the U.S. Attorney's Manual as an individual as to whom the prosecutor already possesses substantial evidence of crimi-

target warnings in the grand jury, either as a matter of state constitutional law or criminal procedure.[27]

In jurisdictions that do *not* require target warnings, the prosecutor must nevertheless take great caution not to *mislead* a grand jury witness about his target status in an effort to lure him into waiving Fifth Amendment protections. ABA Model Rule of Professional Conduct 8.4(c) provides that it is unprofessional for a lawyer to "engage in conduct involving dishonesty, fraud, deceit or *misrepresentation.*" A number of courts have suggested that where a witness or his counsel inquires about the witness's status before the grand jury and is deceived by the prosecutor (e.g., "don't worry, if you cooperate you will be o.k.") the court may in appropriate circumstances dismiss a subsequent indictment issued against the witness, or suppress any evidence provided in reliance on the misleading assurances.[28]

C. Grand Jury Subpoenas

Grand jury subpoenas are issued by the prosecutor on the grand jury's behalf. They are an extraordinarily powerful tool, because they have the power to force the attendance of witnesses who otherwise may be unwilling to cooperate in the government's criminal investigation, and the production of documents that may be undiscoverable through use of a search warrant due to lack of information about their precise scope or where they are kept. Grand jury subpoenas are backed up by the court's power to hold a witness in contempt (for non-compliance) and the prosecutor's power to charge a witness with perjury (for false testimony).

It is improper for a prosecutor to subpoena documents or tangible evidence to the grand jury and then never mark

nal wrongdoing, and a "subject" is defined as a person whose conduct is within the scope of the grand jury's investigation.

27. Pinkerton v. State, 784 P.2d 671, 676 (Alaska App. 1989) (interpreting state constitution); Robinson v. State, 453 N.E.2d 280, 282 (Ind. 1983) (interpreting state statute); Matter of Criminal Investigation, 7th Dist., 754 P.2d 633, 650 (Utah 1988) (interpreting state constitution).

28. *See* United States v. Crocker, 568 F.2d 1049, 1056 (3d Cir. 1977); Commonwealth v. Weed, 17 Mass. App. Ct. 463, 459 N.E.2d 144, 147 (1984). *See also Washington*, 431 U.S. at 188 (test of compulsion under the Fifth Amendment "is whether, considering the totality of the circumstances, the free will of the witness was overborne").

this material as an exhibit for the grand jury's examination.[29] It is also inappropriate for the prosecutor to use the power of a grand jury subpoena for purposes of preparing for trial (for example, to compel the testimony under oath of persons who have been listed on the defendant's trial list as providing an alibi defense). The prosecutor must always keep in mind that grand jury subpoenas may only be used to assist a sitting grand jury in their function of deciding whether and who to indict. The ABA Standards of Criminal Justice provide that "[u]nless the law of the jurisdiction so permits, a prosecutor should not use the grand jury in order to obtain tangible, documentary, or testimonial evidence to assist the prosecutor in preparation for trial of a defendant who has already been charged by indictment or information."[30]

D. Subpoenas to Attorneys

Model Rule of Professional Conduct 3.8(e) restricts the power of a prosecutor to subpoena an attorney to provide information about that attorney's past or present client. Specifically, Rule 3.8(e) provides that a prosecutor shall not "subpoena a lawyer in grand jury or other criminal proceeding to present evidence about a past or present client unless the prosecutor reasonably believes" that 1) the information is not privileged; 2) the information sought from the attorney is essential to the successful completion of an ongoing investigation or prosecution; and 3) there is no other feasible alternative to obtain the information other than through counsel. Although the rule applies to both grand jury and criminal trial subpoenas, disputes over subpoenas served on private attorneys most frequently occur at the grand jury stage of a criminal proceeding.[31]

The attorney-subpoena rule prohibits the government from driving a wedge between a defendant and his counsel

---

29. *See* ABA Criminal Justice Standard 3–3.6(f) (prosecutor should not "abuse the processes of the grand jury."). *See also* Commonwealth v. Cote, 407 Mass. 827, 832, 556 N.E.2d 45 (1990).

30. ABA Criminal Justice Standard 3–3.6(g). *See also* United States v. Woods, 544 F.2d 242, 250 (6th Cir. 1976); United States v. Doe, 455 F.2d 1270, 1273 (1st Cir. 1972). After indict-ment a grand jury subpoena may be utilized to gather additional evidence if the evidence pertains to a superseding indictment, an indictment involving new defendants, or additional crimes. *See* United States Attorney's Manual § 9–11.120.

31. *See* Frank O. Bowman III, *A Bludgeon by Any Other Name*, 9 Geo. J. Legal Ethics 665, 688 (1996).

by attempting to elicit incriminating information about the defendant from his legal representative. Its aim is to prevent the creation of mistrust and conflict of interest that may arise when an attorney is turned into a witness against his client.[32] Depending on the nature and importance of the information sought from counsel, compelling an attorney to testify against a client may implicate Model Rule 3.7 (advocate-witness rule), forcing counsel to withdraw from future representation of the client.[33]

The modern limitation on attorney subpoenas grew out of heightened efforts by prosecutors in the 1980's to combat drug trafficking by aggressively seeking forfeiture of drug proceeds. In the course of investigating the money trail during narcotics forfeiture investigations, prosecutors began to question the source of moneys used to pay attorneys' fees, and sometimes called criminal defense attorneys to testify before the grand jury in order to ascertain the source of their fee payments. Sixth Amendment challenges to such attorney subpoenas on the ground of interference with "right to counsel" were unavailing, because a subject does not have a constitutional right to counsel during the grand jury stage of a criminal investigation.[34] Perceived abuse of attorney subpoenas led a number of states to enact ethical rules addressed to this practice, and the ABA followed the lead of states like Massachusetts and Rhode Island in 1990 by enacting Model Rule 3.8(e)(then numbered 3.8(f)).[35] Eleven states now impose some form of restriction on subpoenas issued to attorneys in criminal investigations.[36]

32. Whitehouse v. United States District Court, 53 F.3d 1349, 1358 (1st Cir. 1995). "From the moment that the subpoena is served on counsel, until the issue of its validity is resolved, the client resides in a state of suspended animation, not knowing whether his attorney will testify against him and perhaps be required to withdraw his representation." *Id*. at 1358. Moreover, service of a subpoena on a target's lawyer "opens a second front which counsel must defend with her time and resources, thus diverting both from the client." *Id*.

33. Judith McMorrow and Daniel Coquillette, THE FEDERAL LAW OF ATTOR-

NEY CONDUCT, § 813.04 (Moore's Federal Practice 2001).

34. *See* In re Grand Jury Subpoenas, 906 F.2d 1485, 1494 (10th Cir. 1990), and cases cited.

35. *See* Stern v. United States District Court, 214 F.3d 4, 8 (1st Cir. 2000).

36. Alaska, Arizona, Colorado, Louisiana, Massachusetts, North Carolina, Oklahoma, Rhode Island, South Carolina, Tennessee and Vermont. *See generally* Fred C. Zacharias, *A Critical Look at Rules Governing Grand Jury Subpoenas of Attorneys*, 76 MINN. L. REV. 917, 917 (1992).

The rule primarily is one of necessity; it expresses a presumption against eliciting information from counsel if the evidence the prosecutor desires is available from other sources. For an attorney-subpoena to be permissible under Rule 3.8(e), the information sought must be non-privileged, highly material, and not available from other sources. Prior to 1995 the ABA Model Rule contained a judicial approval provision, which required a prosecutor to obtain permission from the court following an adversarial proceeding with notice to the effected attorney prior to issuing a subpoena for a lawyer to provide information about a present or former client. However, the judicial approval requirement formerly contained in Model Rule 3.8(f)(2) was removed by the ABA in 1995, largely if not solely for purposes of protecting grand jury secrecy and not allowing a subject of an investigation to be "tipped off" to its scope. A few states have retained the judicial approval requirement in their rules of professional conduct regulating attorney subpoenas.[37] Federal prosecutors have challenged these judicial approval requirements on the grounds that imposing any procedural hurdles on federal prosecutors beyond those imposed by the Federal Rules of Criminal Procedure would violate the Supremacy Clause of the United States Constitution. These challenges have met with varying results at the circuit court level.[38]

37. *See* Mass. R. Prof'l Conduct 3.8(f); R.I. Rule of Prof'l Conduct 3.8(f).

38. In *Baylson v. Disciplinary Board*, the United States District Court for the Third Circuit ruled that enforcement of Pennsylvania Rule 3.10 against federal prosecutors would violate the Supremacy Clause. 975 F.2d 102, 104 (3rd Cir. 1992). The First Circuit later sidestepped the Supremacy Clause issue in *Stern*, 214 F.3d at 17, ruling instead that the Federal District Court exceeded its authority by enacting the Massachusetts version of 3.8(f) as a local federal rule, because the attorney-subpoena requirements imposed new obligations on prosecutors that subverted the purpose of the Federal Rules of Criminal Procedure (particularly Rule 17 regarding standards on motions to quash subpoenas).

The Tenth Circuit upheld a state attorney subpoena rule against Supremacy Clause challenge in *United States v. Colorado Supreme Court*, 189 F.3d 1281 (10th Cir. 1999), ruling that the former Colorado disciplinary rule requiring advance judicial approval of attorney subpoenas was enforceable against federal prosecutors. The discrepancy between the *Baylson* and *Colorado* outcomes can be explained by the interim enactment of the McDade Amendment in 1998. Entitled "Ethical Standards for Attorneys for the Government," the McDade Amendment provides that that federal attorneys "shall be subject to state laws and rules...governing attorneys in each State where such attorney engages in that attorney's duties, to the same extent and in the same manner as other attorneys in that State." Pub. L. No.

Notably, the attorney-subpoena rule restricts the ability of prosecutors to subpoena counsel to the grand jury even if the lawyer-witness represented the subject in a *civil* rather than a criminal matter. For example, unless the prerequisites of Rule 3.8(e) have been met, a prosecutor investigating an alleged bank fraud in connection with a target's real estate purchases would be restricted from subpoenaing the target's former real estate counsel to testify about the land transactions, or to produce records relating to these contracts. So long as the matter presently under investigation is a criminal matter, the rule imposes restrictions on subpoenaing an attorney to provide information about his client, irrespective of whether the attorney represented the client in a civil or criminal matter, and irrespective of whether the matter was litigation related or transactional in nature.

E. Exculpatory Evidence

A controversial issues in the area of prosecutorial ethics is whether a government lawyer should inform the grand jury of evidence favorable to the target of the investigation. Prior inconsistent statements made by police officers and eyewitnesses, scientific test results that suggest that someone other than the target may have committed the crime, and testimony from alibi witnesses placing the target at a location other than the crime scene on the date and time in question are all examples of "exculpatory evidence" the grand jury might find useful in deciding whether to indict a prospective defendant. As will be discussed in Chapter 5, once a defendant is indicted he has a constitutional right to discover such helpful evidence in the hands of the government. Withholding evidence favorable to the accused after indictment violates the defendant's due process rights because it deprives him of an opportunity to prepare for trial.[39]

There are strong arguments for imposing a similar disclosure obligation on prosecutors earlier in the criminal

---

105–277, § 801(a), 112 Stat. 2681–119 (codified at 28 U.S.C. § 530B). Since Congress expressly allowed the states to enact ethical rules governing the conduct of federal attorneys practicing in their jurisdictions, and since the Tenth Circuit construed the Colorado attorney subpoena rule as essentially an "ethical" rule, the court found no Supremacy Clause violation. *See* 189 F.3d at 1288.

39. Brady v. Maryland, 373 U.S. 83, 86 (1963).

proceedings, and requiring them to inform the grand jury of any evidence favorable to the accused. First, the grand jury may be unable to exercise their screening function adequately and weed out weak cases if they are not informed of evidence that exonerates the accused or mitigates the degree of his offense. Second, if the prosecutor's overriding duty is to insure that "justice" is done, he should take reasonable steps to insure that the grand jury does not return an indictment against an innocent person. A faulty indictment not only causes irreparable injury to the named defendant but also wastes the resources of the court system.

On the other hand, there are countervailing policy arguments in favor of limiting a prosecutor's disclosure obligations before the grand jury. First, a duty to inform the grand jury of evidence favorable to the accused is inconsistent with the grand jury's minimal role of gauging only whether there is "probable cause" to believe that the defendant has committed a crime. Second, interposing disclosure obligations at the grand jury level would turn these abbreviated charging proceedings into "mini-trials," thereby consuming scarce judicial and prosecutorial resources.

A prudent prosecutor should make the grand jury aware of highly probative evidence that would completely exonerate the potential target, because shielding this evidence from the grand jury would cause an indictment to issue in a case that probably cannot be proven beyond a reasonable doubt at trial. However, there are less substantial and probative forms of exculpatory evidence (e.g., a prior inconsistent statement by a grand jury witness) that are not likely to justify enlarging and prolonging the grand jury's inquiry. The question of where to draw the line between favorable information that should be disclosed to the grand jury and favorable information that may be withheld by the prosecutor and simply turned over the defendant for use at a trial has dogged courts and commentators.[40] This question strikes at the core of the grand jury's independence as a deliberative body; if a prosecutor is aware of evidence that exonerates the target but withholds this evidence from the grand jury, then

40. *See* R. Michael Cassidy, *Toward a More Independent Grand Jury: Recasting and Enforcing the Prosecu-* *tor's Duty to Disclose Exculpatory Evidence,* 13 GEO. J. LEGAL ETHICS 361, 368 (2000).

the grand jury is hearing only a one-sided presentation of the facts.

For federal prosecutors, this question was resolved in the case of *United States v. Williams*, wherein the United States Supreme Court ruled that a prosecutor has no constitutional or common-law duty to present exculpatory evidence to the grand jury, and that federal courts have no authority to impose such an obligation on prosecutors pursuant to their general superintendence powers.[41] After *Williams*, federal prosecutors have no legal duty whatsoever to reveal exculpatory evidence at the grand jury stage of a criminal proceeding—including substantially exculpatory evidence such as forensic tests that reveal that someone else may have committed the crime in question (e.g., DNA, fingerprints) or recantation of the principal complaining witness. A small number of states have followed this federal approach.[42]

Some state courts, acting pursuant to their supervisory authority over the grand jury, have declined to follow the *Williams* approach. These courts have imposed an obligation on prosecutor's to disclose to the grand jury "substantial" exculpatory evidence that "directly negates" the guilt of the target.[43] In some state jurisdictions, whenever evidence is so important that it might reasonably cause the grand jury not

41. United States v. Williams, 504 U.S. 36, 54 (1992). The Court in *Williams* virtually eliminated a federal court's authority over a prosecutor's conduct in the grand jury. The Court held that because the grand jury is an institution separate from Article III courts, a federal court is not free to fashion rules of grand jury practice under its general superintendence power. *Id.* at 50. After *Williams*, a federal court can dismiss an indictment for misconduct in the grand jury only where the prosecutor violates a clear constitutional provision, statute, or formally enacted rule of criminal procedure, and even then only where this violation provides the court with "grave doubt" that the grand jury would have indicted absent the misconduct. *Id.* at 46 and 54 (*citing* Bank of Nova Scotia v. United States, 487 U.S. 250, 256 (1988)). Moreover, the subsequent conviction or guilty plea of a defendant indicted on the basis of an improper grand jury proceeding insulates the indictment from challenge under federal harmless error doctrine. United States v. Mechanik, 475 U.S. 66 (1986).

42. People v. Pulgar, 323 Ill.App.3d 1001, 256 Ill.Dec. 705, 752 N.E.2d 585, 592 (2001); State v. Easter, 661 S.W.2d 644, 645 (Mo. Ct. App. 1983); In re Grand Jury Proceedings, 129 S.W.3d 140, 143 (Tex. Ct. App. 2003).

43. *See, e.g.,* Commonwealth v. Connor, 392 Mass. 838, 467 N.E.2d 1340, 1351 (1984); State v. Hogan, 144 N.J. 216, 676 A.2d 533, 543 (1996); People v. Lancaster, 69 N.Y.2d 20, 511 N.Y.S.2d 559, 503 N.E.2d 990, 993 (1986).

to indict the target, it must be revealed to the tribunal by the prosecutor.

While the Model Rules of Professional Conduct do not specifically address this difficult question,[44] the standard of "substantiality" followed by many state courts is advocated by the drafters of certain ethical guidelines for prosecutors. The United States Attorney's Manual cautions federal prosecutors that in the interests of justice they should disclose exculpatory evidence to the grand jury whenever they are "personally aware of substantial evidence that directly negates the guilt of [the] subject."[45] This standard distinguishes between seriously exculpatory evidence that would undermine the guilt of the target (e.g., alibi evidence, negative scientific test results, recantation by the sole eye-witness) and other favorable but less substantial evidence (e.g., prior inconsistent statements by government witnesses, self serving post-arrest statements made by the target himself, etc.). The former should be disclosed to the grand jury, but the latter need not be since they do not "directly negate" guilt. A similar accommodation is echoed in both the NDAA Standards[46] and the ABA Criminal Justice Standards.[47]

A third approach to the problem of exculpatory evidence before the grand jury is to let the target of the investigation appear and tell his side of the story. Some states have attempted to insure a more balanced presentation of evidence before the grand jury by enacting statutes that afford a putative defendant the right to appear before the grand jury and to testify under oath if he chooses.[48] States which follow this "right to appear" approach risk tipping the defendant off to an upcoming criminal indictment, and the flight that may ensue.[49] In the federal system, the prosecutor

44. *See* ABA Model Rule 3.8(a) (prosecutor shall "refrain from prosecuting a charge that the prosecutor knows is not supported by probable cause").

45. U.S. Attorney's Manual § 9–11.233.

46. *See* NDAA Standard 58.4.

47. ABA Criminal Justice Standard 3–3.6(b).

48. *See* Nev. Rev. Stat. § 172.241 (2003); N.Y. Crim. Proc. Law § 190.50(5)(a)(2004).

49. New York requires the prosecutor to give the target notice of his statutory right to appear before the grand jury only in those cases where the target has already been arraigned on similar felony charges in local criminal court. N.Y. Crim. Proc. Law § 190.50(5)(a). Nevada allows the prosecutor to petition the court for

is not obligated to give the target of a grand jury investigation the right to appear and testify, although the U.S. Attorney's Manual advises federal prosecutors to give "favorable consideration" to a target's request to appear before the grand jury.[50]

F. Grand Jury Secrecy

The prosecutor may not disclose what transpires before the grand jury to the media, to civil lawyers, to legislative or administrative bodies, or to any member of the public at large. What happens in the grand jury room—including both the deliberations of the jurors and the specific testimony of the witnesses—is secret, and may not be disclosed to anyone other than a government official participating in the investigation and prosecution of the case.[51] Government lawyers, their agents, the stenographer, and the jurors themselves are all subject to this strict rule of secrecy. By contrast, witnesses appearing before the grand jury (and their counsel where counsel is permitted in the grand jury room) are *not* subject to secrecy restrictions. They are free to talk to the press (or other lawyers and witnesses) about the grand jury investigation and/or their testimony before this body.

Federal Rule of Criminal Procedure 6(d)—like analogous rules operating in many states—provides that "A person performing an official function in relation to the grand jury may not disclose matters occurring before the grand jury except in the performance of his official duties or when specifically directed to do so by the court." Although arguably not a matter "occurring before the grand jury," for pragmatic reasons a prosecutor should be hesitant even to confirm that a grand jury investigation has been *commenced*, or the precise scope of the grand jury's inquiry.

The Supreme Court has recognized several justifications for the "long established policy" of maintaining the secrecy

permission to withhold notice where the defendant is a flight risk or poses a danger to the life or property of others. Nev. Rev. Stat. § 172.241(3)(a).

50. U.S. Attorney's Manual § 9–11.152.

51. *See* Fed. R. Crim. P. 6(e)(3)(A)(ii) (allowing disclosure to any government agent "that an attorney for the government considers necessary to assist in performing that attorney's duty to enforce federal criminal law").

of grand jury proceedings.[52] The rules of secrecy prevent the escape of those whose indictment may be imminent; they insure the grand jury freedom from attempted influence; they discourage subornation of perjury or tampering with witnesses who may be called to testify before the grand jury; they encourage full and free disclosures by persons subpoenaed; and, they protect innocent persons from suffering unnecessary damage to their reputation should they *not* be indicted at the end of the inquiry.

To prevent leaks and guard against improper influence, local rules of criminal procedure typically limit who may be present in the grand jury room during the presentation of evidence.[53] Under Federal Rule 6(d)(1), only the lawyer or lawyers participating in the presentation of the evidence to the grand jury, the witness, an interpreter for the witness (if necessary), and the stenographer are authorized in the grand jury room. Some state rules of criminal procedure are slightly less restrictive than their federal counterpart; in addition to the foregoing persons, some states authorize the presence of "any persons necessary or convenient to the presentation of the evidence."[54] In these states, the prosecutor may allow in to the grand jury room a victim-witness advocate if necessary to comfort or support a distraught witness, or a financial investigator if reasonably necessary to aid the prosecutor in the presentation of complex evidence. State jurisdictions that allow for the attendance of persons who are "reasonably necessary" to the presentation of evidence typically do not require court approval prior to allowing such persons inside the grand jury room; however, a prosecutor who allows a non-lawyer into the grand jury

---

52. United States v. Procter & Gamble Co., 356 U.S. 677, 682 n. 6 (1958), *citing* United States v. Rose, 215 F.2d 617, 628–29 (3d Cir. 1954).

53. United States v. Mechanik, 475 U.S. 66, 70 (1986) (where rule prohibiting presence of unauthorized persons in the grand jury is violated, dismissal is not automatic; court must determine whether defendant was substantially prejudiced). Rule 6(d) and its state counterparts were designed, in part, "to ensure that grand jurors, sitting without the direct supervision of a judge, are not subject to undue influence that may come with the presence of an unauthorized person." *Id.*

54. Mass. R. Crim. P. 5(c). *See* Nev. Rev. Stat. § 172.235 (2004) (authorizing presence of "[a]ny other person requested by the grand jury"); N.Y. Crim. Proc. Law § 190.25 (McKinney 2004)(authorizing presence of interpreters, audio visual operators, prison transportation officials, and any mental health professional providing emotional support to child witness).

room during the presentation of evidence runs the risk that his decision may later be challenged on a motion to dismiss the indictment.

Where a transcript is made of grand jury proceedings, many jurisdictions require that the prosecutor turn over part or all of the grand jury minutes to counsel for any defendant indicted by the grand jury, in order to assist the defendant in preparing his defense.[55] Prosecutors may also share these grand jury transcripts with other prosecutors in their office, and with any police officers, civilian employees and victim-witness advocates assisting them with a grand jury presentation or the subsequent prosecution (that is, the "case team").[56] But rules of grand jury secrecy may preclude a prosecutor from sharing grand jury material with a lawyer employed by the government in a civil capacity. For example, in the course of investigating a crime a prosecutor may uncover evidence of civil infractions that he wishes to refer to external administrative agencies such as the Internal Revenue Service, the Environmental Protection Agency, the Immigration and Naturalization Service, etc. Rule 6(e) of the Federal Rules of Criminal Procedure—like its analogue in many states—allows a prosecutor to disclose grand jury material to "an attorney for the government for use in performing that attorney's duty." However, the Supreme Court in *United States v. Sells Engineering, Inc.*[57] rejected the government's contention that this so-called "official duty" exception to the grand jury secrecy rule allows a prosecutor, as a matter of right, to share grand jury material with *other* public officials for the performance of *their* official duties, limiting the "duty" language of Rule 6(e) to the prosecutor's duty to enforce federal *criminal* law. The Court ruled that where a federal prosecutor seeks to share grand jury material with a public officer other than those participating directly in a federal criminal investigation (in that case, an attorney for the Civil Division of the Department of Justice preparing a civil tax fraud case), the prosecutor must first convince the judge presiding over the grand jury that

55. *Cf.* 18 U.S.C. § 3550(e)(3) (Jencks Act requires prosecutor to turn over only those portions of grand jury minutes containing testimony of those witnesses who testify at trial).

56. *See, e.g.,* Fed. R. Crim. P. 6(e)(3)(A)(ii).

57. 463 U.S. 418 (1983).

there is a "particularized need" for disclosure that out-
weighs the need for grand jury secrecy.[58] In making this ex
parte determination of "particularized need," the court will
consider the other government lawyer's need for the information, their ability to obtain it from other sources, the
importance of the parallel civil investigation, and the risks of
leaks presented by disclosure.[59] Not all state courts that
utilize grand juries have followed the *Sells Engineering*
decision, and some have "official duty" exceptions to their
grand jury secrecy rules that are broader than Fed. R. Crim.
P. Rule 6(e).[60] State prosecutors should be mindful of the
specific language used in their jurisdiction's pertinent rule of
criminal procedure before sharing grand jury material with
any other government agencies.

The aforementioned rules of grand jury secrecy apply
only to testimony and other matters occurring *before* the
grand jury. They do not prohibit prosecutors from disclosing
documents that were presented to the grand jury and gath-
ered pursuant to a grand jury subpoena, so long as these
documents were prepared outside the grand jury and not
specifically for purposes of the grand jury's investigation
(e.g. pre-existing business records, written correspondence,
etc.). At least in the federal courts, such pre-existing documents are not considered "grand jury matters" to which the
rules of secrecy apply, even if the documents are shown to a
witness and are the subject of examination and testimony
inside the grand jury room.[61]

G. "Off-the-Record" Comments
by Prosecutor

The prosecutor is authorized to act as legal advisor to
the grand jury.[62] He may properly instruct them on the
elements of crimes under investigation, and answer any legal

---

58. *Id.* at 442.

59. *Id.* at 445. Notably, Fed. R.
Crim. P. 6(e)(3) specifically allows a
federal prosecutor, without judicial
permission, to disclose grand jury material to a federal prosecutor in a different district for use in another
criminal investigation, and to disclose
foreign intelligence information
learned in the grand jury to any federal law enforcement, department of
defense, or national security official.

See In re Impounded Material, 277
F.3d 407 (3d Cir. 2002).

60. *See, e.g.,* Ariz. Rev. Stat. § 13–
2812; Mass. R. Crim. P. 5(d).

61. *See, e.g.,* SEC v. Dresser Indus-
tries, Inc., 628 F.2d 1368, 1381–84
(D.C. Cir. 1980); United States v.
Johns, 688 F.Supp. 1017 (E.D. Pa.
1988).

62. ABA Criminal Justice Standard
3–3.5(a).

questions they have about the evidence. However, the prosecutor must avoid stating his personal opinions about the evidence, the credibility of any witnesses, or the strength of the charges. Both the ABA Criminal Justice Standards and the NDAA Standards caution that a "prosecutor should not make statements or arguments in an effort to influence grand jury action in a manner which would be impermissible at trial before a petit jury."[63] The following types of remarks by prosecutors in the grand jury room may be considered to undermine the grand jury's status as an "independent legal body:"[64] denigrating a witness's assertion of a Fifth Amendment privilege,[65] commenting on a witness's retention of counsel or the motives of counsel,[66] suggesting to the grand jury how to interpret certain evidence,[67] commenting on the credibility of a witness,[68] and discussing unproven prior criminal activity of the defendant.[69]

A defendant's ability to challenge the prosecutor's conduct before the grand jury, including the nature or sufficiency of the evidence and the regularity of the proceedings, depends on there being an adequate record (usually a stenographic transcript) of what transpired in the grand jury room. It is inappropriate for the prosecutor to instruct a stenographer to "go off the record" when he is eliciting testimony from a witness or counseling the grand jury. The ABA Standards provide that "the prosecutor's communications and presentations to the grand jury should be on the record."[70] The only discussions in the grand jury room which may be conducted "off the record" are the deliberations of the jurors, the results of their votes, and any discussions relating purely to administrative matters such as scheduling,

---

63. ABA Criminal Justice Standard 3–3.5(b); NDAA Standard 60.3.

64. NDAA Standard 60.2.

65. *See* United States v. Benjamin, 852 F.2d 413, 420–21 (9th Cir. 1988); United States v. Duff, 529 F.Supp. 148, 155 (N.D. Ill. 1981).

66. United States v. DiGregorio, 605 F.2d 1184, 1189 (1st Cir. 1979).

67. United States v. Breslin, 916 F.Supp. 438, 443 (E.D. Penn. 1996).

68. United States v. Sears, Roebuck & Co., 518 F.Supp. 179, 186 (C.D. Cal. 1981), *rev'd on other grounds*, 719 F.2d 1386 (9th Cir. 1983).

69. *Id.*

70. ABA Criminal Justice Standard 3–3.5 (c).

recesses, attendance of future witnesses, etc.[71] Some courts have ruled that it is improper for a prosecutor to fail to record the instructions of law which he reads to the grand jury,[72] although this presently appears to be an open issue in many jurisdictions.[73]

Problems

1. Assistant District Attorney Pamela Hunt is prosecuting an armed robbery case. The defendant is held in the dock awaiting a bail argument and arraignment. He is being interviewed by his appointed public defender in preparation for the court proceeding. Suddenly, the prisoner gets angry and pulls a home-made knife out of his sock, stabbing the public defender in the neck. Court officers rush in and subdue the prisoner. The public defender is transported to the hospital, where he undergoes surgery and survives the attack. ADA Hunt is assigned to prosecute the defendant on the additional charge of armed assault on the public defender with intent to kill him. May the prosecutor subpoena the public defender to the grand jury to testify about the attack?

2. Assistant United States Attorney Nadine Pellegrini is investigating a stock broker for securities fraud and embezzlement from clients. The prosecutor subpoenas several of the broker's former clients to the grand jury. She discovers that one of these clients has a prior conviction for perjury. If the witness testifies before the grand jury in a way that inculpates the target, does the prosecutor have a duty to advise the grand jury about the witness' previous perjury conviction? If the witness testifies to the grand jury in a manner different from a prior statement which he made to an FBI agent, does the prosecutor have an obligation to bring the witness' prior inconsistent statement to the attention of the grand jury?

a. During the same grand jury presentation, a witness finishes testifying and leaves the room. A grand juror asks the prosecutor "Did that witness say something different from the previous witness?" Is Mr. Target a registered "stockbroker" or a registered "investment advisor?" May the prosecutor answer the grand juror's question? What if the grand juror had asked "Why

71. *See, e.g.,* Fed. R. Crim. P. 6(e) ("Except when the grand jury is deliberating or voting, all proceedings must be recorded by a court reporter or by a suitable recording device.").

72. *See, e.g.,* Wilkey v. Superior Court, 115 Ariz. 526, 566 P.2d 327,

329 (1977); People v. Percy, 45 A.D.2d 284, 358 N.Y.S.2d 434, 435 (1974).

73. Bennett L. Gershman, PROSECUTORIAL MISCONDUCT, § 2:26 at p. 2–36 (2d ed. 2003).

can't these victims just sue civilly to get their money back?" May the prosecutor answer that question, and if so how?

b.   One week before the prosecutor's grand jury presentation is scheduled to conclude, the prosecutor receives a letter from the stock broker's counsel stating that "Mr. Target has in his possession reams of documentary evidence which exculpate him from the charges which you are investigating. Mr. Target would like to appear before the grand jury, tell his side of the story, and explain these documents." Does the prosecutor have an obligation to present the documents to the grand jury? To allow the target to appear before the grand jury and testify?

c.   One day before the grand jury is scheduled to vote, the prosecutor receives information that the target has a fifth personal bank account about which the prosecutor was previously unaware. Can the prosecutor issue a grand jury subpoena to the bank for the records of this account, even though she knows that the bank will not be able to deliver the requested documents to her office until after the grand jury has finished its work on the case?

Chapter Four

Contacting and Interviewing Witnesses

A prosecutor must conduct interviews with witnesses to a crime in order to assess the strengths and weaknesses of the case, to fill evidentiary gaps presented by the available police reports, and to prepare for trial. Often these interviews and trial preparation sessions will occur in the courthouse during a break in the proceedings. For more complex cases, however, these interviews may be arranged in advance and take place in the prosecutor's office at a mutually convenient time. In either scenario, there are a variety of ethical considerations that a prosecutor must bear in mind before meeting with and interviewing witnesses.

First, a prosecutor may not compel the witness to attend an interview through the color of a subpoena. Witnesses have a right to talk to the prosecutor or not to talk to the prosecutor out of court, at their option. There is no legal requirement that they cooperate with a government lawyer's extra-judicial request for information. Subpoenas are properly issued to command a witness's attendance at court proceedings (e.g., pre-trial hearing, grand jury, or trial) if the prosecutor anticipates a need for their testimony. While it is not inappropriate for a prosecutor to subpoena a witness to court with the intent to interview the witness prior to their planned testimony, it is inappropriate for a prosecutor to issue a subpoena to compel a witness to attend a trial or pre-trial proceeding with full knowledge that the witness will not be called to testify—that is, where the prosecutor wishes simply to use the subpoena as a pretext to convince a reluctant witness to present themselves for an interview. A small minority of jurisdictions authorize a prosecutor to issue so-called "administrative" or "investigative" subpoenas to conduct trial preparation.[1] Unless the prosecutor is working in one of these jurisdictions, it is inappropriate to issue a subpoena for the sole purpose of facilitating witness interviews. The ABA Criminal Justice Standards provide that "[a] prosecutor should not secure the attendance of persons for interviews by use of any communication which has the appearance or color of a subpoena or similar judicial process unless the prosecutor is authorized by law to do so."[2]

As a matter of both professional ethics and sound trial strategy, a prosecutor should never interview an important civilian witness alone.[3] The prosecutor may wish to create a record of the witness's statements, in the event that the witness changes his story on the witness stand and the prosecutor needs to impeach the witness with his earlier statement. If the prosecutor were the only witness to such an interview and needed to take the stand himself to complete the impeachment, it is likely that a mistrial would be declared and the prosecutor would be precluded from continuing in the prosecution role due to the prohibition of an attorney in a case also serving as a witness in the same proceeding.[4] For these reasons, a prosecutor should ask a police officer, a civilian investigator employed by his office, or a victim-witness advocate to be present when the prosecutor interviews a critical witness. While this may not always be practical in routine misdemeanor cases prosecuted in the district courts, it is certainly advisable in major felony cases, and in all cases where the prosecutor suspects that the witness may change his story due to fear or improper influence.

It is unprofessional conduct for a prosecutor to counsel or assist a witness to testify falsely.[5] The prohibition on procuring perjured testimony derives from the obligation of

1. *See* H. Morely Swingle, *Criminal Investigative Subpoenas: How to Get Them, How to Fight Them*, 54 J. Mo. B. 15 (1998). *See, e.g.,* Fla. Stat. Ann. § 27.04 (2004); Kan. Stat. Ann. § 22–3101 (2003).

2. ABA Criminal Justice Standard 3–3.1(e).

3. *See* ABA Criminal Justice Standard 3–3.1(g) (A prosecutor should "avoid interviewing a prospective witness except in the presence of a third person" unless he is "prepared to forego impeachment... by the prosecutor's own testimony ... or to seek leave to withdraw from the case.")

4. *See* ABA Model Rule 3.7.

5. ABA Model Rule 3.4(b).

candor to the judicial tribunal, which all attorneys share. A prosecutor must be uniquely sensitive to the power he holds in the criminal justice system, and the tendency many civilian witnesses might have to look to the prosecutor for guidance or suggestions on how to testify. The prosecutor's goal during a witness interview should be to *draw out* facts from the witness—not to *implant* or *suggest* facts as true that the prosecutor has no way of objectively verifying. The practice of "horseshedding" a witness—that is, suggesting that the witness testify in a particular manner and then rehearsing that scripted testimony—must be scrupulously avoided. While it is not improper for a prosecutor to advise the witness on courtroom demeanor and presentation skills, or even to suggest to the witness that he or she use certain language in conveying the witness's version of pertinent facts, the prosecutor should at all times be mindful that it is the *witness's* version of events that controls. The prosecutor must avoid any attempt to strong-arm a witness to testify in a particular fashion.[6]

It is improper for a prosecutor to impede the defendant's access to witnesses. Factual witnesses do not "belong" to either party in a criminal case. The defendant has a right to attempt to interview a witness the government intents to call at trial, if the witness wishes to be interviewed. While the witness may decline to be interviewed by the defense team, that is the witness's choice, and not the prosecutor's.[7] Thus, a prosecutor should never advise a witness not to talk to the defendant, his counsel, or an investigator for the defendant.[8] Such obstruction of the defendant's access to witnesses is not only an ethical violation, it may also be considered a violation of the defendant's due process rights.[9] A prosecutor who is concerned about witness safety

---

6. *See* ABA Model Rule 3.4(b), Comment 1. *See also* Michael S. Ross, *Thinking Outside the Box: How the Enforcement of Ethical Rules Can Minimize the Dangers of Prosecutorial Leniency and Immunity Deals*, 23 CARDOZO L. REV. 875, 884 (2002).

7. United States v. Matlock, 491 F.2d 504, 506 (6th Cir. 1974).

8. *See* ABA Criminal Justice Standard 3–3.1(d) (prosecutor should not advise or cause any person "to decline to give the defense information which such person has a right to give"). *See also* United States v. Cincotta, 689 F.2d 238, 245 (1st Cir. 1982). *Cf.* ABA Model Rule 3.4(a) ("A lawyer shall not...*unlawfully* obstruct another party's access to evidence") (emphasis supplied).

9. *See, e.g.,* United States v. Bell, 506 F.2d 207, 223 (D.C. Cir. 1974); Davis v. Lehane, 89 F.Supp.2d 142, 149 n.6 (D. Mass. 2000).

and intimidation may make a request of the witness that the prosecutor be informed of and allowed to attend any interview between that witness and a representative of the accused, so long as the prosecutor makes clear to the witness that whether and under what circumstances the witness submits to an interview with the defense team is the witness's choice alone.

In jurisdictions that require the prosecutor to disclose in pre-trial discovery the address of any anticipated government witnesses, it is not improper for the prosecutor—where it is concerned about the safety of a particular witness—to list that witness's address as "care of" the prosecutor's office (e.g., an informant or a cooperating accomplice). In such circumstances, however, the court may require the prosecutor to make the witness available for a pre-trial interview with defense counsel at the prosecutor's office. During that meeting, the witness is free to inform defense counsel that he does not wish to discuss the case, and promptly terminate the interview.[10]

A. Communicating with Unrepresented Persons

Because the prosecuting attorney is viewed as a source of authority and power in the criminal justice system, it is not uncommon for a witness in a criminal case to ask a prosecutor for legal advice. For example, a victim of theft may ask the prosecutor about possible civil remedies, a victim of domestic violence may ask the prosecutor for guidance in divorce or child custody proceedings, and an ordinary witness to a crime may seek the prosecutor's guidance with pending immigration problems. The prosecutor must be mindful that 1) their area of legal expertise is typically confined to criminal matters, and to advise a witness about collateral legal issues may be performing a disservice to that witness; and 2) at times the witness's interest and the government's interest may *not* coincide. In those situations, the provision of legal advice by the prosecutor to an unrepresented witness could be riddled with actual or

---

10. *See, e.g.,* United States v. Walton, 602 F.2d 1176, 1179 (4th Cir. 1979).

potential conflict of interest. For these reasons, the Rules of Professional Conduct require that wherever there is a "reasonable possibility" of an unrepresented person's interests being in conflict with the interests of the lawyer's client, the lawyer "shall not give legal advice" to that unrepresented person "other than the advice to secure counsel."[11] Moreover, a prosecutor may not state or imply that he is disinterested when in fact the prosecutor has an objective that may conflict with the objective of an unrepresented witness. Where the prosecutor perceives that the witness is confused about the prosecutor's role, the prosecutor has an affirmative duty to "make reasonable efforts to correct the misunderstanding."[12]

The ethical rule restricting a lawyer's provision of legal advice to an unrepresented person has direct application to a prosecutor's relationship with a criminal defendant where that defendant decides to proceed *"pro se"* (that is, as his own counsel). This scenario frequently arises in cases involving misdemeanor charges in district courts where the defendant represents himself. Although the prosecutor is allowed to talk directly to a *pro se* defendant,[13] he may never give legal advice to a *pro se* defendant, because the interests of a criminal defendant and those of the prosecutor are always in potential conflict. The only advice that a prosecutor may give to a *pro se* defendant is the advice to secure his own legal counsel.[14] While Comment [2] to Rule 4.3 authorizes a prosecutor to negotiate a disposition of charges with an unrepresented defendant following the waiver of counsel in open court,[15] in the course of such negotiations the prosecutor must scrupulously avoid providing the unrepresented accused with legal advice about the advisability or conse-

---

11. ABA Model Rule 4.3.

12. *Id.*

13. The restrictions of the "no-contact" rule prohibiting the prosecutor from talking directly to a criminal defendant without his counsel's permission do not apply to defendants proceeding *pro se,* because the defendant and his counsel are one in the same entity.

14. ABA Model Rule 3.8(c) also prohibits a prosecutor from seeking to

obtain from an unrepresented accused a waiver of important pre-trial rights, such as the right to an indictment or preliminary hearing.

15. ABA Model Rule 4.3, Comment [2] ("This Rule does not prohibit a lawyer from negotiating the terms of a transaction or settling a dispute with an unrepresented person."). *See also* ABA Model Rule 3.8(c), Comment [2]; ABA Criminal Justice Standard 3–4.1(b).

quences of the defendant's actions (e.g., employment, licensing, or immigration consequences of a guilty plea).

B. Communicating with Represented Persons: The "No–Contact" Rule

The "no-contact" rule forbids an attorney from communicating with a person represented by counsel on the subject of that representation without the permission of the witness's attorney. In effect, when a person is known to be represented in a matter, the attorney must first go through their counsel for permission to interview that witness. All fifty states contain a "no-contact" provision in their attorney conduct rules,[16] although state rules vary in terminology. ABA Model Rule 4.2 provides as follows:

> In representing a client, a lawyer shall not communicate about the subject of the representation with a person the lawyer knows to be represented by another lawyer in the matter, unless the lawyer has the consent of the other lawyer or is authorized to do so by law or a court order.

The purposes of the "no-contact" rule are threefold: 1) to encourage professional courtesy by requiring permission before one lawyer talks to another lawyer's client; 2) to prevent a lawyer, through overreaching and/or superior bargaining power, from tricking a witness into making damaging admissions or concessions without their lawyer's knowledge; and 3) to discourage uncounseled waivers of the attorney-client privilege.[17]

The proper application of the "no-contact" rule in criminal cases has been the subject of extensive and at times acrimonious debate among the defense bar, the Department of Justice, and state and local bar disciplinary authorities.[18] The defense bar has argued that the rule imposes restrictions on prosecutors beyond those imposed by constitutional protections. Specifically, they point to the Fifth Amendment

16. *See* Bruce A. Green, *Whose Rules of Professional Conduct Should Govern Lawyers in Federal Court and How Should the Rules be Created?*, 64 GEO. WASH. L. REV. 460, 471 (1996).

17. *See* ABA Model Rule 4.2, Comment [1].

18. For an excellent summary of the history of the no-contact rule and the debate surrounding its application in criminal cases, *see* Green, *supra* ch. 4 n.16, at 470–479.

(which has been interpreted to prohibit custodial interrogations of a witness without affording them an opportunity to have counsel present),[19] and the Sixth Amendment (which provides a criminal defendant with a right to counsel once criminal proceedings have been initiated, and prohibits the state from interfering with that relationship by "deliberately eliciting" admissions from the defendant without his counsel being present).[20] Unlike the Fifth and Sixth Amendment guarantees, which are waivable by the holder of the right (the client), the protections of the "no-contact" rule are waivable only by the witness's attorney. The "no-contact" rule is thus a potential source of limitation on the government's right to conduct criminal investigations which otherwise fully comport with constitutional safeguards.

In 1995, the American Bar Association amended Model Rule 4.2 to prohibit communications with a represented *"person"* without the consent of that person's lawyer.[21] As previously drafted, the pertinent ethical rule—derived from former Model Code provision DR 7–104(a)—applied the "no-contact" limitation only to represented *"parties."* A number of jurisdictions—including Arizona, California, the District of Columbia, and Illinois—have retained the former version of the rule, and limit the application of their no-contact provision to "parties" represented by counsel.[22] As discussed below, the uncertainties presented by application of the "no-contact" rule in the criminal context are substantially diminished in jurisdictions which proscribe contact with represented "parties" rather than represented "persons." This is a rapidly developing area of the law; prosecutors should be mindful of the particular language used in their jurisdiction's no-contact rule, and of any advisory notes or judicial opinions explicating the rule's application in the criminal context.

Where a prosecutor violates the no-contact rule, the likely sanction is that the court will either hold the prosecutor in contempt or refer the errant prosecutor to bar disci-

---

19. Miranda v. Arizona, 384 U.S. 436 (1966).

20. *See* Maine v. Moulton, 474 U.S. 159, 176 (1985) ("The Sixth Amendment guarantees the accused, at least after the initiation of formal charges,

the right to rely on counsel as a 'medium' between him and the State.").

21. Gillers and Simon, REGULATION OF LAWYERS at 266 (Aspen 2004).

22. *Id.* at 268–271 and 865.

plinary authorities for appropriate sanction. Most courts have ruled that suppression of evidence or dismissal of the indictment are prices too high to pay for violation of ethical as opposed to constitutional norms, and thus have refused to apply exclusionary rules to violation of no-contact prohibitions.[23]

1. Represented Parties

At its core, in jurisdictions which proscribe conduct with represented *"parties,"* the "no-contact" rule prohibits prosecutors from speaking with a charged defendant without his counsel either being present or consenting to the interview. A prosecutor thus cannot have a conversation with a defendant in the courthouse lobby without counsel's permission— even if the defendant initiates the contact. A defendant who approaches a prosecutor after a court session and asks for information about his case, or asks to speak with the prosecutor about future proceedings, or seeks voluntarily to reveal information to the prosecutor about the circumstances of the crime, must be unequivocally told by the prosecutor that the prosecutor cannot speak to the defendant without his lawyer's permission. Simply put, a prosecutor must avoid all private contact on the subject of the representation with a defendant who is represented by counsel.[24] Similarly, a prosecutor cannot *indirectly* contact the defendant, such as by writing him a letter proposing a plea bargain, or copying the defendant on a letter sent by the prosecutor to defense counsel, without also running afoul of the "no-contact" rule.

In jurisdictions which prohibit contact with represented "parties," the "no-contact" rule imposes one significant obligation on prosecutors which exceeds the requirements of the Sixth Amendment. On occasion, a defendant may wish to cooperate with the government without his lawyer's knowledge (that is, by providing the government with information about the criminal activities of others). Cooperating defendants may wish to proceed without their attorney's knowl-

23. *See* United States v. Lopez, 4 F.3d 1455, 1464 (9th Cir. 1993); People v. Green, 405 Mich. 273, 293, 274 N.W.2d 448 (1979); State v. Ciba–Geigy Corp., 247 N.J.Super. 314, 589 A.2d 180 (1991).

24. The government may continue to have contact with a defendant with respect to its investigation of uncharged crimes, so long as the communication is not on the subject matter of the pending charges. *See* Hoffa v. United States, 385 U.S. 293, 308 (1966).

edge when they fear for their personal safety if persons close to a criminal enterprise learn of their informant status. The right to counsel provision of the Sixth Amendment would not forbid a defendant from meeting privately with the government in this scenario, because the Sixth Amendment protection is a right of the *accused* which may be waived by the accused. However, the "no-contact" rule prohibits contact with the defendant without his *lawyer's* consent unless the prosecutor is "authorized to do so by law or a court order." Under the "no-contact" rule, a prosecutor cannot talk to a defendant who initiates a conversation about cooperation and waives the presence and advice of his attorney, unless the defendant either obtains a new attorney, or unless the prosecutor obtains judicial permission to talk to the defendant without counsel being present. The advisable course for a prosecutor in these situations is to privately take the defendant before a judge and to have the court determine in a closed, *ex parte* proceeding whether 1) the defendant knowingly and voluntarily waives his right to counsel for the purposes of the requested interview; and 2) whether allowance of the interview without the defendant's lawyer's consent is consistent with the purposes and policies behind the "no contact" rule.[25]

Where a prosecutor has charged a corporation with a crime (e.g., an environmental crime, a health care fraud violation, etc.) a question often arises as to which employees of the corporation are considered "parties" represented by corporate counsel for purposes of the "no-contact" rule. Once the corporation has been indicted, must the prosecutor and his investigative agents avoid conducting interviews with *any* corporate employees without the permission of corporate counsel? Application of the no-contact rule in the corporate context raises particularly difficult issues because corporations are non-physical entities who may only act through individuals. A broad reading of the rule would severely limit law enforcement's ability to collect information from corporate employees who may have knowledge of the events at issue. State and federal courts have taken

---

25. *See, e.g.,* United States v. Lopez, 4 F.3d 1455, 1461 (9th Cir. 1993) (while court order may justify contact with represented party in situations where defendant wishes to cooperate without his lawyer's knowledge, order was not valid in this case where prosecutor mislead court about facts during *ex parte* proceeding).

widely differing views on this complex issue. Some jurisdictions have taken a narrow view, ruling that only high-level executives who are members of the corporate "control group" directing the litigation are off-limits to interviews without corporate counsel's assent.[26] Other courts have taken the much broader view that *any* corporate employee whose statement would be binding on the corporation as an admission (generally an employee making a statement about activities within the scope of his corporate duties) is represented by corporate counsel for purposes of the "no-contact" rule.[27] A middle-ground approach, essentially that recommended by the American Bar Association in its 2002 Comments to Model Rule 4.2, would forbid contact with three classes of corporate employees absent permission of corporate counsel: 1) employees whose acts or omission are directly at issue in the litigation; 2) employees who have management or supervisory authority over the allegedly unlawful acts or omissions; and 3) high-level executives who have authority to bind the corporation with respect to the course of the litigation (i.e., the control group).[28] Most courts that have confronted the issue have ruled that *former* employees of the corporation are not automatically represented by corporate counsel for purposes of the "no-contact" rule.[29] A prosecutor may thus interview former employees without first obtaining the permission of the attorney for the corporation, unless that former employee has specifically retained corporate counsel to represent him and the fact of that representation is known to the prosecutor.

2. *Represented Persons*

In jurisdictions where the "no-contact" rule prohibits conduct with represented "persons,"[30] the implications of

26. *See, e.g.,* Fair Automotive Repair, Inc. v. Car–X. Serv. Sys., Inc., 128 Ill.App.3d 763, 84 Ill.Dec. 25, 471 N.E.2d 554, 561 (1984); Wright v. Group Health Hospital, 103 Wash.2d 192, 691 P.2d 564, 569 (1984).

27. *See, e.g.,* Weibrecht v. Southern Ill. Transfer Inc., 241 F.3d 875, 883 (7th Cir. 2001); Brown v. St. Joseph County, 148 F.R.D. 246, 254 (N.D.Ind. 1993).

28. ABA Model Rule 4.2, Comment [7]. *See* Messing, Rudavsky & Weliky, P.C. v. President and Fellows of Har-

vard College, 436 Mass. 347, 764 N.E.2d 825, 833 (2002); Niesig v. Team I, 76 N.Y.2d 363, 559 N.Y.S.2d 493, 558 N.E.2d 1030 (1990).

29. Clark v. Beverly Health and Rehabilitation Services, 440 Mass. 270, 797 N.E.2d 905, 912 (2003) (collecting authorities). *See* ABA Model Rule 4.2, Comment [7] ("Consent of the organization's lawyer is not required for communication with a former constituent.")

30. For example, Alaska, Connecticut, Massachusetts, Pennsylvania, and

Rule 4.2 for criminal proceedings are far more ambiguous and complex. At a minimum, a prosecutor must adhere to the prohibitions on contacting represented parties, discussed above. They must also go through counsel for permission to contact any ordinary witness who retains a lawyer to advise the witness during a criminal proceeding. But the hardest questions under the "no contact" rule arise in situations where the *target* of the investigation retains defense counsel prior to being charged by indictment or complaint. The concern of government lawyers in these situations is that suspects can impede routine and constitutional investigatory methods (e.g., informant penetration, police interviews) simply by "lawyering up" at an early stage of a criminal investigation. Whether and how the "no-contact" rule imposes obligations on a prosecutor beyond those imposed by the Fifth and Sixth Amendments with respect to their contact with represented targets in the pre-charging setting is hotly debated issue subject to widespread controversy.[31] In fact, one federal judge has described this area as "an unsettled judicial wilderness."[32]

At least three difficult questions present themselves for prosecutors in jurisdictions where the "no contact" rule applies to represented "persons." First, may prosecutors and their investigative agents continue to conduct undercover operations on a suspect prior to charging but after the suspect has "lawyered-up?" For example, the government may be investigating an unsolved murder, and may be focusing its attention on the victim's boyfriend. In situations where the suspect hires a lawyer to represent him during the criminal investigation, may the prosecutor and the police attempt to record conversations between a willing informant and the suspect on the subject of the crime? In a Formal

Texas apply their no-contact rule to represented "persons." *See* Gillers and Simon, *supra* Intro. n. 2, at 268–70.

31. The United States Department of Justice is so concerned that the vagaries of the "no-contact" rule will impede the legitimate investigatory work of federal prosecutors that it has supported recent initiatives to repeal the McDade Amendment's requirement that federal prosecutors comply with state ethical rules. *See* Justice Enhancement and Domestic Security Act, Senate Bill 22 § 4503(b) (2003).

32. In re Criminal Investigation of John Doe, Inc., 194 F.R.D. 375, 378 (D. Mass 2000).

Opinion, the ABA has taken the position that pre-charging undercover contacts with a represented person in a criminal investigation are not prohibited by the "no-contact" rule.[33] The vast majority of courts that have addressed this issue have similarly ruled that the "no-contact" rule does not prohibit lawful undercover activities directed at a target of a criminal investigation after he has retained counsel (e.g., conversations with "wired" informants, attempts by undercover officers to purchase contraband, etc.). Some courts have based this conclusion on a determination that undercover operations are "authorized by law" so long as they comport with Fourth and Fifth Amendment guarantees and any applicable statutory restraints on searches and electronic surveillance, reasoning that the "no-contact" rule was not intended to restrict the government's ability to ferret out crime through accepted investigative techniques.[34] Other courts have based this conclusion on the pragmatic recognition that the "no-contact" rule prohibits communication "about the subject of the representation" when the person is known to be represented "in the matter;" in a pre-charging context, the "matter" has not fully crystalized so that the government has an ability to discern the precise scope of the lawyer's representation and act accordingly.[35] The only federal court that has prohibited undercover contacts with represented persons did so on the ground that the government engaged in misconduct during the undercover investigation (that is, issued a fake subpoena to encourage conversations by the target with an undercover informant) and therefore the contact was not deemed by that court to be "authorized by law."[36]

A second difficult question for prosecutors operating in jurisdictions which prohibit contact with represented "persons" is whether the police may interview a suspect prior to

33. ABA Formal Opinion 95–396.

34. *See, e.g.,* United States v. Kenny, 645 F.2d 1323, 1339 (9th Cir. 1981); United States v. Grass, 239 F.Supp.2d 535, 539 (M.D. Pa. 2003), and cases cited.

35. *See, e.g.,* United States v. Lemonakis, 485 F.2d 941, 955 (D.C. Cir. 1973).

36. United States v. Hammad, 858 F.2d 834, 840 (2d Cir. 1988) ("the use of informants by government prosecutors in a pre-indictment, non-custodial situation, absent the type of misconduct that occurred in this case, will generally fall within the 'authorized by law' exception").

arraignment[37] without permission of his counsel. Such an "over-the-counter" (as opposed to "undercover") communication would not be prohibited by the Fifth Amendment, so long as the interview takes place in circumstances where the defendant is not in custody (e.g., where the police visit the suspect at his home). Even where the defendant is in custody (e.g., upon arrest), if the defendant waives his right against self incrimination following the receipt of proper warnings, the Fifth Amendment is not violated where he voluntarily agrees to talk to the police without his counsel being present.[38] Does the no-contact rule proscribe police interviews in either of these two situations? Most courts that have addressed this issue have concluded that it does not, although their reasoning is often conflicting. Courts have ruled variously that pre-charging police interviews are "authorized by law;"[39] that the parameters of the "matter" in which the defendant is represented have not yet crystallized,[40] and—although less common—that the "no-contact" rule has no application whatsoever to pre-indictment criminal investigations.[41]

Another basis for upholding constitutionally acceptable pre-arraignment police interviews is that the police are simply not covered by Rule 4.2. That is to say, the "no-contact" rule is an ethical rule for *lawyers*, and only lawyers are bound by its provisions. Therefore, police who interview a represented suspect outside the presence of the suspect's attorney are not violating Rule 4.2. Nevertheless, lawyers have responsibility for adequately supervising investigators who are employed by their office, and may not "order or ratify" conduct of a non-lawyer employee that would be incompatible with the professional obligations of the lawyer.[42] Moreover, even for police officers not directly employed by the prosecutor's office, Model Rule 8.4(a) states that it is

---

37. The Sixth Amendment right to counsel does not attach until the formal initiation of criminal charges—generally the issuance of a criminal complaint, information, or indictment. *See* Brewer v. Williams, 430 U.S. 387, 398 (1977).

38. Miranda v. Arizona, 384 U.S. 436 (1966).

39. *See, e.g.,* United States v. Balter, 91 F.3d 427, 435 (3rd Cir. 1996).

40. *See, e.g.,* In re Disciplinary Proceedings Regarding John Doe, 876 F.Supp. 265, 268 (M.D. Fla. 1993).

41. *See, e.g.,* United States v. Sutton, 801 F.2d 1346, 1366 (D.C. Cir. 1986).

42. ABA Model Rule 5.3(c).

unprofessional conduct for a lawyer to "knowingly assist or induce another to [violate the rules of professional conduct], or *do so through the acts of another*."[43] This section would arguably prohibit a prosecutor from directing a police officer to interview a subject whom the prosecutor knew to be represented by counsel. An application of the "no-contact" rule to pre-indictment police interviews could have the unintended consequence of causing prosecutors to decline to take an active role in directing pre-indictment investigations. So long as the prosecutor is not viewed as directing, assisting, or ratifying the conduct of police, he will not be held responsible for a police officer's contact with a represented person.

Is it permissible for a prosecutor to participate directly in a pre-arraignment interview with a represented target? For example, if a represented suspect is arrested and waives the presence of counsel after being given his *Miranda* warnings, may the prosecutor join the police in the interrogation room and participate in the interview? Those courts which hold that the "no-contact" rule has no application to criminal investigations prior to the initiation of formal charges would have no trouble in upholding such attorney contact.[44] But several courts have distinguished between pre-charging *police* interviews and pre-charging interviews conducted by *prosecutors*, on the grounds that 1) attorneys have superior bargaining power to the accused due to their training and expertise, and 2) the prosecutor can always manipulate the timing of a criminal complaint or indictment, and thereby circumvent the "no-contact" rule.[45] Prosecutors who participate in pre-charging interviews with a represented suspect without their lawyer's permission should do so with extreme caution, and only after consulting controlling disciplinary authority in their particular jurisdictions.[46] At a minimum,

---

43. Justice Department regulations implementing the no-contact rule following the enactment of the McDade Amendment provide that prosecutors "shall not direct an investigative agent acting under the attorney's supervision to engage in conduct under circumstances that would violate the attorney's obligations." 28 CFR § 77.4 (2004).

44. *See Balter*, 91 F.3d at 435; State v. Porter, 210 N.J.Super. 383, 510 A.2d 49, 54 (1986).

45. *See* United States v. Foley 735 F.2d 45, 49 (2d Cir. 1984); United States v. Ward, 895 F.Supp. 1000, 1006–07 (N.D. Ill. 1995).

46. In submissions to the Ethics 2000 Committee, the Department of Justice took the position that a prosecutor should be allowed to participate

they should avoid using the opportunity of an ex parte interview to negotiate a pre-charging plea bargain with a represented suspect, which is strongly discouraged under ABA Criminal Justice Standard 3–4.1(b).[47]

Most jurisdictions that prohibit contact with represented persons provide an exception for communications that are "authorized by law." In addition to lawful undercover activities, the following types of contacts have generally been considered "authorized by law" where expressly contemplated by local statute or rule of criminal procedure: service of a subpoena; execution of a search warrant at the premises of the represented person; and examination of the witness in the grand jury room pursuant to lawfully executed process.[48]

Problems

1.   Assistant District Attorney Molly Parks is prosecuting a shoplifting charge in district court. The defendant appears competent and articulate. At arraignment, he elects to proceed without counsel. After he has signed a waiver of counsel and filed this waiver in open court, the prosecutor and the defendant have a hallway discussion about the possible disposition of the criminal charges. The prosecutor indicates a willingness to continue the charges without a finding upon restitution and the payment of court costs. The defendant asks the prosecutor whether this will result in him having a "criminal record" such that he can be deported. (He admits that he is in the country illegally.) How should the prosecutor respond?

in an interview of an arrested suspect without his counsel present, so long as the suspect is given his Miranda warnings and voluntarily waives his Fifth Amendment rights. The ABA Committee specifically rejected that argument, and modified Comment [5] of Rule 4.2 to provide that "[t]he fact that a communication does not violate a state or federal constitutional right is insufficient to establish that the communication is permissible under this Rule." According to one participant in the drafting committee, this addition to the comments was intended to "preclude the notion than an ex parte communication with a represented person is permitted at the time of arrest mere-ly because the represented person waives the constitutional right to consult counsel." Carl A. Pierce, *Variations on a Basic Theme: Revisiting the ABA's Revision of Model Rule 4.2* (Part III), 70 TENN. L. REV. 643, 665 (2003).

47. "A prosecutor should not engage in plea discussions directly with an accused who is represented by defense counsel, except with defense counsel's approval."

48. *See* United States v. Schwimmer, 882 F.2d 22, 28 (2d Cir. 1989) (grand jury testimony); Mass. Rule Professional Conduct 4.2 Comment [1] (service of process).

2.   Prosecutor Carol Starkey is investigating ABC Corp., a water treatment facility, for knowingly causing a discharge of pollutants into a nearby river in a manner which posed a risk to public health. She has commenced a grand jury investigation, and has subpoenaed certain records from the corporation pertaining to their business. A prominent defense lawyer calls the prosecutor on the phone and indicates that he has been retained by the corporation for purposes of the criminal investigation. The lawyer states that he represents the corporation "and all current and former corporate employees." He demands that the prosecutor not talk to any employees without seeking his permission first. He also demands that all future subpoenas to the corporation or its employees be directed to him. Is the prosecutor free to send out investigators to interview corporate employees who may have witnessed the discharge? To serve subpoenas on them?

3.   Assistant District Attorney Judy Zeprun has indicted two individuals for cocaine trafficking. One defendant was the supplier of cocaine, the other merely a delivery person, or "mule." Following the arraignment, the supplier posts $100,000 cash bail and is released. The mule is unable to post bail, and is held awaiting trial. Two weeks after arraignment, the investigating officer informs the prosecutor that he has received a call from the mule from jail. The mule says he is ready to "turn" on his supplier. The mule states that in addition to cocaine trafficking, the supplier is a gun runner. The mule states that if the government agrees to a reduction of bail so he can get out of jail, the mule is willing to introduce an undercover officer to the supplier to enable him to purchase guns. The mule says he does not want his lawyer to know about his cooperation, because his lawyer is being paid by the supplier. Can the prosecutor send the police officer to the jail to "debrief" the mule? Can the government send the mule, once he gets out of jail, to meet the supplier for the purposes of setting up a further sting?

4.   An Independent Counsel appointed by the United States Court of Appeals is investigating current and former White House officials for bank fraud and obstruction of justice. Contemporaneous with this investigation, the President of the United States is defending himself in a civil lawsuit charging him with sexual harassment. The allegation in the civil lawsuit is that the President demanded sexual favors from a state employee while he was serving as a state governor. Lawyers for the plaintiff in the sexual harassment suit subpoena a White House intern to inquire about a possible sexual relationship she may have had with the President. Represented by counsel, the intern provides a sworn affida-

vit in the civil case denying that she had a sexual relationship with the President. However, at the same time, the intern is recorded having private conversations with a former colleague at the White House bragging about just such a relationship, and stating that she was urged to lie about the affair in her affidavit. The intern's colleague agrees to cooperate with the Independent Counsel's office, and to wear a wire to a meeting with the intern at a local Washington hotel. After the intern makes further statements secretly recorded on tape suggesting that she had perjured herself in her affidavit about her relationship with the President, she is confronted at the hotel by FBI agents and Assistant Special Prosecutors. They seek to convince her that "the gig is up" and that she should cooperate with their criminal probe of the White House. Is such a meeting between the intern and the Assistant Special Prosecutors without the intern's civil lawyer being present a violation of the "no-contact" rule?

CHAPTER FIVE

PROVIDING TIMELY DISCOVERY
TO THE ACCUSED

Perhaps the most critical obligation of a prosecutor is to provide the defense counsel with discovery about the charges so that he can adequately prepare his client's defense. "Discovery" in the criminal context can mean several things. First, state and federal rules of criminal procedure typically set forth a list of materials that must be provided by the prosecutor to defense counsel. This list typically includes notification of the date and place of the offense, the names and addresses of anticipated trial witnesses, copies of the grand jury minutes, any written or recorded statements of witnesses, copies of pertinent police reports, results of scientific tests and analyses, and access to (i.e., right to inspect) any physical or documentary evidence the government intends to introduce at trial.[1] Local rules of criminal procedure also typically provide a timeframe for production of these materials (e.g., thirty days before trial). A judge confronted with a prosecutor who disregards discovery rules may impose case-based sanctions on the government, such as excluding the proffered but previously undisclosed evidence, granting the defendant a continuance to allow him to inspect the material, or, in extreme circumstances, holding the prosecutor in contempt for violation of a rule of criminal procedure or court order.[2]

---

[1] *See, e.g.,* Cal. Penal Code § 1054.1 (West 2004); Mass. R. Crim. P. 14(a); N.Y. Crim. Proc. Law § 240.20(1).

[2] *See* Bank of Nova Scotia v. United States, 487 U.S. 250, 263 (1988).

Discovery contemplated by the pertinent rules of criminal procedure mostly concerns so-called "inculpatory" evidence; that is, evidence that the prosecutor intends to use to link the defendant to the crime. However, the prosecutor also has a legal and ethical duty to disclose to the defendant any "exculpatory" evidence in its possession; that is, evidence that is helpful to the defendant because it could be used to prove that that the defendant *did not* commit the alleged offense. In other words, a prosecutor must not only reveal the government's case to the defendant, he must also disclose any evidence that will help the defendant build his case. In this regard, the prosecutor's duty of disclosure is much broader than defense counsel's, because a lawyer for the accused has no general obligation to reveal to the prosecutor evidence in its possession which may help prove his client's guilt.[3]

Exculpatory evidence can come in a variety of forms. Statements by witnesses giving a description of the perpetrator which does not match the defendant, inability of an eyewitness to identify the accused from a photo array or lineup, inconsistent statements given on previous occasions by key government witnesses, scientific test results that are inconclusive or negative, and an admission of responsibility by an accomplice are all examples of exculpatory evidence which must be revealed to the defense. "Exculpatory evidence" has been defined as any evidence that "provides some significant aid to the defendant's case, whether it furnishes corroboration of the defendant's story, calls into question a material, although not indispensable, element of the prosecution's version of the events, or challenges the credibility of a key prosecution witness."[4]

The duty to disclose exculpatory evidence is central to the prosecutor's obligation as a minister of justice. Unlike a

3. In Williams v. Florida, the Supreme Court ruled that a limited duty imposed by a state rule of criminal procedure that required the defendant to disclose to the prosecutor in advance of trial the names and addresses of any alibi witnesses did not violate the defendant's Fifth Amendment privilege against self incrimination, although the court suggested that a more extensive discovery obligation requiring disclosure by the defendant of *inculpatory* material might run afoul of that protection. 399 U.S. 78, 81 and 86 (1970). *Cf.* ABA Criminal Justice Standard 4–4.5 ("Defense counsel should make a reasonably diligent effort to comply with a legally proper discovery request.").

4. Commonwealth v. Ellison, 376 Mass. 1, 379 N.E.2d 560, 571 (1978).

defense attorney, whose duty is to represent his client's interests vigorously within the bounds of the law,[5] the prosecutor's duty is to seek the *truth*; presenting only a one-sided version of facts while withholding evidence helpful to the accused undermines the prosecutor's obligation of fairness and impartiality. While some prosecutors may fear that their case will be "jeopardized" if they reveal evidence helpful to the accused, this concern is based on an overly narrow and shortsighted view of the prosecutor's role. Although the prosecutor must advocate strenuously to make sure that the guilty do not escape punishment, he has an equal if not greater responsibility to ensure that the innocent are not convicted.

Moreover, the government typically has greater resources than the accused and greater access to sources of information. The power to subpoena testimony and the production of documents, the power to direct the investigation of police officers, the power to immunize witnesses, and the natural affinity which crime victims feel for the government understandably result in the prosecutor having greater access to information than the defendant. Requiring prosecutors to disclose exculpatory evidence to the accused reflects not only a difference between the prosecutor's and defense counsel's respective missions,[6] but also the fact that the prosecutor typically is in a better position than defense counsel to receive and to process information about the alleged crime.

The prosecutor's duty to disclose exculpatory evidence to the accused has both constitutional and ethical dimensions. In *Brady v. Maryland*,[7] the Supreme Court ruled that "the suppression by the prosecution of evidence favorable to an accused upon request violates due process...."[8] The court likened the withholding of exculpatory evidence by the prosecutor to the knowing presentation of perjured testimony, which it had previously declared to violate the due process clause in *Mooney v. Holohan*.[9] According to the Court, "[a] prosecution that withholds evidence on demand of an accused which, if made available, would tend to exculpate him

5. *See* ABA Model Rule 1.2(a).
6. Green, *supra* ch. 1, n.2 at 620.
7. 373 U.S. 83 (1963).
8. *Id.* at 87.
9. 294 U.S. 103 (1935).

or reduce the penalty helps shape a trial that bears heavily on the defendant. That casts the prosecutor in the role of an architect of a proceeding that does not comport with standards of justice....”[10]

Nine years later, the Court in *Giglio v. United States* enlarged its construction of constitutionally “exculpatory” evidence to encompass evidence which would demonstrate a witness's bias towards the government.[11] Under *Giglio*, the government must disclose to the defendant any promises, rewards, or inducements made to a government witness in exchange for his testimony—whether these inducements are written or oral, formal or informal. Promises to assist witnesses with criminal or civil matters pending against them, offers to pay them money or relocation expenses, agreements to assist them with outstanding probation matters or deportation proceedings, promises not to prosecute them for their role in the crime, and assurances that their cooperation will be made known to the court at time of sentencing are all examples of “promises, rewards and inducements” that must be disclosed to the defense under *Giglio*.[12] The fact that the proposed reward to the witness may be conditional on the prosecutor's satisfaction with the witness's performance at trial,[13] or that the inducement is made to the attorney for the witness rather than to the witness himself,[14] does not detract from the government's obligation to disclose the promise or reward.

---

10. *Brady*, 373 U.S. at 87–88.

11. Giglio v. United States, 405 U.S. 150, 155 (1972).

12. R. Michael Cassidy, *Soft Words of Hope: Giglio, Accomplice Witnesses, and the Problem of Implied Inducements*, 98 NORTHWESTERN U. L. REV. 1129 (2004).

13. United States v. Bagley, 473 U.S. 667, 683 (1985) (fact that the promised payment “was expressly contingent on the Government's satisfaction with the end result, served only to strengthen any incentive to testify falsely in order to secure a conviction”); Brown v. Wainwright, 785 F.2d 1457, 1464 (11th Cir. 1986) (promise of non-prosecution for accomplice conditioned upon his passing polygraph must be disclosed under *Giglio*).

14. *See* Campbell v. Reed, 594 F.2d 4, 6 (4th Cir. 1979) (finding *Giglio* violation where state made promise of non-prosecution to accomplice's lawyer, and lawyer merely told witness that “everything would be all right.”); Burkhalter v. State, 493 S.W.2d 214, 216–17 (Tex. Crim. App. 1973) (lawyer told by prosecutor that if accomplice to murder did not invoke or request immunity he would not be prosecuted as accomplice; lawyer did not tell his client but just told him that “it could help him”), *cert. denied*, 414 U.S. 1000 (1973).

In addition to promises, rewards and inducements to government witnesses that may reveal bias, *Brady* and its progeny require a prosecutor to disclose to the defendant any evidence that may be used to impeach a government witness on a material point of his testimony.[15] For example, evidence that a witness has given a prior statement inconsistent with his trial testimony on a key issue,[16] or instances of prior acts of dishonesty on the part of the witness that could be used to attack the witness's character for truthfulness under Fed. R. Evid. 608(b),[17] must all be turned over to the defense, assuming that the witness's testimony is central enough to the prosecution's case that the nondisclosure of such impeachment information would be considered constitutionally "material," as discussed below.

Although the Court's decision in *Brady* referenced the prosecutor's constitutional duty to turn over exculpatory evidence "on request" of the defendant, subsequent cases have recognized that this constitutional duty of disclosure exists whether or not the defendant specifically requested the withheld material, only generally requested exculpatory information, or filed no discovery requests at all.[18] In other words, the prosecutor's duty to turn over evidence favorable to the accused is *self executing;* it does not depend on the presence or precision of discovery requests filed by defense counsel. Elemental fairness requires disclosure of all *Brady* and *Giglio* material, even in the absence of a request, because counsel for the defendant may not know whether such evidence exists or what form it might take sufficient to file an appropriately tailored discovery motion.

The due process clause may also be violated where a prosecutor or the police destroy evidence that *potentially* may have been exculpatory, before the importance or significance of the evidence can be assessed. In *California v. Trombetta*[19] the Court addressed a claim that the police had destroyed samples of breath taken from the defendant dur-

---

15. *Bagley*, 473 U.S. at 676 (rejecting any constitutional distinction between impeaching information and exculpatory evidence).

16. *See, e.g.,* United States v. Carter, 313 F.Supp.2d 921, 925 (E.D. Wis. 2004).

17. *See, e.g.,* United States v. Kelly, 35 F.3d 929, 936 (4th Cir. 1994).

18. *Bagley*, 473 U.S. at 682; United States v. Agurs, 427 U.S. 97, 107 (1976).

19. 467 U.S. 479 (1984).

ing a breathalyzer examination following his arrest for operating under the influence. The defendant alleged that if his breath sample had been preserved, the defendant could have conducted a subsequent reanalysis and pointed out any defects in the government's equipment or technique. The court rejected this argument, noting that the potential exculpatory value of the sample was speculative, and that the police had destroyed the breath samples pursuant to normal operating procedure. Nonetheless, the court noted that destruction of evidence by the government might in other circumstances lead to a due process violation where two conditions are established; first, that the potential exculpatory value of the evidence was "apparent [to the government] before the evidence was destroyed," and second, that the defendant was "unable to obtain comparable evidence by other reasonably available means."[20] In *Arizona v. Young-blood*,[21] the Court clarified its *Trombetta* ruling, specifically assigning the defendant the burden of establishing *bad faith* on the part of the government in destroying potentially exculpatory evidence. Under this line of cases, examples of constitutionally impermissible destruction of exculpatory evidence may include deporting a witness who the defendant intends to call at trial to establish his innocence,[22] and authorizing destruction of a fetus aborted from a rape victim before it could be tested to establish paternity.[23]

Following the lead of *Brady*, Rules of Professional Conduct enacted in most states also impose an affirmative ethical obligation on prosecutors to disclose exculpatory evidence to the accused prior to trial. ABA Model Rule of Professional Conduct 3.8(d) requires a prosecutor to "make timely disclosure to the defense of all evidence or information known to the prosecutor that tends to negate the guilt of the accused or mitigates the offense." The vast majority of states have adopted language in their attorney conduct rules that mirrors or closely tracks this "tends to negate guilt" definition of exculpatory evidence.[24] For reasons discussed

20. *Id.* at 489

21. 488 U.S. 51, 58 (1988).

22. *See* United States v. Valenzuela–Bernal, 458 U.S. 858, 873 (1982).

23. *See* Commonwealth v. Sasville, 35 Mass. App. Ct. 15, 616 N.E.2d 476, 481 (1993).

24. *See* Richard A. Rosen, *Disciplinary Sanctions Against Prosecutors*

below, the use of the term *"tends"* in Rule 3.8(d) and its predecessor, ABA Model Code provision DR 7–103(b), was likely intended to suggest a broader disclosure obligation than the "materially exculpatory evidence" standard of *Brady* and its progeny. [25]

With respect to nondisclosed (as opposed to destroyed) evidence, neither the ethical rule nor the constitutional duty hinge on the motive of the prosecutor. As the Court specifically ruled in *Brady*, due process if violated where evidence favorable to the defendant is withheld by the prosecutor, "irrespective of the good faith or bad faith of the prosecution."[26] Similarly, under Rule 3.8(d), the ethical duty of disclosure attaches so long as the exculpatory evidence is "known to the prosecutor." There is no *mens rea* requirement under the Model Rule: so long as the evidence was known to the prosecutor, it does not matter whether he understood or appreciated the exculpatory significance of the material. Whether the prosecutor fails to turn over exculpatory evidence due to negligence (e.g., the press of an overwhelming workload), for benevolent purposes (e.g., to protect the privacy of a victim) or for a more malevolent reason (e.g., to gain a tactical advantage) is simply irrelevant under either ABA Model Rule 3.8 or *Brady*. Only a small number of jurisdictions have deviated from the ABA Model Rule by imposing a state of mind requirement before a prosecutor may be disciplined for nondisclosure of exculpatory evidence.[27]

The due process standard and the ethical rule are also similar in that they require a "timely" disclosure of exculpatory evidence. Although Rule 3.8 does not define what "timely" means in the context of either the rule or the

---

for Brady Violations: A Paper Tiger, 65 N.C. L. REV. 693, 715 n.122 (1987).

25. *See* American Bar Association, MODEL RULES OF PROFESSIONAL CONDUCT: PROPOSED FINAL DRAFT, Committee note to Rule 3.8 at 157–58 (May 30, 1981). *Cf.* American Bar Association, STANDARDS FOR CRIMINAL JUSTICE, Comment to Standard 3–3.11 p. 82 (3d ed. 1993) (noting that obligation of prosecutor to disclose exculpatory evidence "goes be-

yond the corollary duty imposed upon prosecutors by constitutional law").

26. 373 U.S. at 87.

27. *See* Ala. R. Prof'l Conduct 3.8(d) (prosecutor shall not "willfully" fail to disclose exculpatory evidence); D.C. R. Prof'l Conduct 3.8 (e) (prohibiting "intentional" failure to disclose); Va. R. of Prof'l Conduct 3.(d) (requiring prosecutor to disclose evidence which he "knows" tends to negate guilt of accused).

commentary, cases interpreting *Brady* have focused on whether the material was delivered to the defendant in time for him to make effective use of it at trial.[28] The ABA Criminal Justice Standards, by contrast, encourage a prosecutor to disclose exculpatory evidence to the defendant "at the earliest feasible opportunity."[29] This aspirational standard suggests that it is improper for a prosecutor to delay the disclosure of exculpatory evidence for tactical advantage.

The constitutional disclosure rule and the ethical obligation apply equally to the guilt and the punishment phases of a criminal proceeding. A prosecutor who is aware of evidence that mitigates the potential punishment must disclose it to the defendant. *Brady* itself was a case where the undisclosed evidence (an accomplice's confession to being the actual shooter in an admitted joint venture) was relevant not to the guilt or innocence of the accused, but only to whether the defendant would be subject to capital punishment or life in prison. The Supreme Court ruled that a prosecutor must disclose to defense counsel all evidence material to "the guilt or punishment" of the defendant.[30] ABA Model Rule 3.8(d) similarly requires the prosecutor, "in connection with sentencing," to disclose all "unprivileged mitigating information known to the prosecutor." These provisions are especially important in jurisdictions which follow a sentencing guideline system, where the judge is required to sentence the defendant to a term of imprisonment within a predefined range unless he finds the presence or absence of mitigating or aggravating circumstances. Any circumstance of the crime known by the prosecutor to be "mitigating" must be disclosed to the defense.

Notwithstanding the similarities noted above, the disclosure obligations of Rule 3.8 and *Brady* diverge in several important respects. Perhaps most obviously, there are different consequences for breach of the constitutional disclosure obligation versus the ethical duty. If the court finds a violation of due process, the remedy is typically either declaration of a mistrial (if the withheld evidence is discovered

28. Leka v. Portuondo, 257 F.3d 89, 99–100 (2d Cir. 2001); Patler v. Slayton, 503 F.2d 472, 478–79 (4th Cir. 1974).

29. ABA Criminal Justice Standard 3–3.11(a).

30. Brady v. Maryland, 373 U.S. at 87.

during the proceedings and a continuance cannot cure any prejudice to the accused) or ordering a new trial (if the jury has already returned a guilty verdict). On rare occasions, a court confronted with a *Brady* violation during trial may also rectify the government's misconduct by precluding the prosecutor from making use of any *inculpatory* evidence relating to the exculpatory material withheld.[31] By contrast, sanctions for a violation of the Rules of Professional Conduct are imposed against the *attorney*, not against the *case*; the range of remedies available to a bar disciplinary authority may include a reprimand, suspension, or disbarment of the prosecuting attorney. One commentator has noted that in the criminal area—where prosecutorial misconduct offends both constitutional and ethical prescriptions—bar disciplinary authorities too frequently defer to case-based sanctions, perhaps in the naïve belief that sanctions imposed by courts will act as a more potent deterrent to prosecutorial misconduct than professional discipline.[32] The result is that bar oversight of prosecutors for failing to disclose exculpatory evidence in criminal cases is relatively rare.

The constitutional and ethical disclosure obligations also differ in how important or significant the evidence needs to be in order to render nondisclosure a breach. To make out a *Brady/Giglio* violation, a defendant must establish that 1) the prosecution suppressed evidence, either willfully or inadvertently; 2) the evidence was favorable to the accused; and 3) the evidence was material.[33] Evidence will be considered "material" within the meaning of *Brady/Giglio* only "if there is a reasonable probability that, had the evidence been disclosed to the defense, the result of the proceeding would have been different."[34] Three issues a court will typically

31. *See, e.g.,* United States v. Campagnuolo, 592 F.2d 852, 858 (5th Cir. 1979).

32. *See* Rosen, *supra* ch. 5 n. 24 at 732–33.

33. Strickler v. Greene, 527 U.S. 263, 281–82 (1999). In *Strickler,* the court highlighted the importance of the materiality element of *Brady,* stressing that the withholding of exculpatory evidence is not a true *Brady* error in the absence of prejudice. *Id.* at

281 ("strictly speaking, there is never a real '*Brady* violation' unless the nondisclosure was so serious that there is a reasonable probability that the suppressed evidence would have produced a different verdict.").

34. *Bagley,* 473 U.S. at 682. In *Bagley,* the Court adopted a uniform standard of materiality to be applied to all instances of undisclosed evidence, irrespective of whether the evidence withheld was specifically requested by the defendant, only generally request-

examine in order to determine whether undisclosed evidence was material under *Brady* are: 1) the importance of the evidence withheld; 2) the strength of the government's case aside from the exculpatory material; and 3) other sources of defense available and utilized by the defendant.[35] Due to this high standard of materiality, a prosecutor may withhold evidence favorable to the accused and still not be in violation of the due process clause, if the withheld evidence is not considered to be so important that it would have likely effected the outcome of the case. In contrast, the pertinent ethical rule requiring disclosure by prosecutors of exculpatory evidence is not limited to "material" evidence; in fact, Model Rule 3.8(d) does not use the word "material" at all. Model Rule 3.8(d) requires prosecutors to turn over to the defense any information that "tends to negate the guilt" of the accused.[36] Whereas *Brady* looks at the *probable* effect of the evidence on the outcome of the proceeding, Model Rule 3.8(d) looks at the evidence's *tendency* to effect the outcome, seeming to contemplate a slightly looser standard.

In another critical respect, however, the constitutional disclosure obligation is more rigorous than the ethical rule. Due process requires exculpatory evidence to be revealed whenever it is "possessed by the prosecutor or anyone over whom the prosecutor has authority."[37] For purposes of the constitutional safeguard, facts known to the *police* will be imputed to the prosecutor for *Brady* purposes, whether or not the prosecutor has actual knowledge of them. The Supreme Court in *Kyles v. Whitley* imposed an affirmative duty

---

ed, or not requested at all. *Id.* at 682. The Supreme Court later clarified the *Bagley* definition of materiality in *Kyles v. Whitley*, stating that the reviewing court need not decide whether the evidence, if disclosed, would have established innocence, but rather "whether in its absence [defendant] received a fair trial, understood as a trial resulting in a verdict worthy of confidence." 514 U.S. at 434.

35. *See* Bennett L. Gershman, PROSECUTORIAL MISCONDUCT §§ 5.5–5.7 (West 2003).

36. An earlier version of this ethical mandate in the Code of Professional Responsibility used the same "tends to negate... guilt" language. *See* MOD-EL CODE OF PROF'L RESPONSIBILITY DR 7–103(b) (1973).

37. Whether an investigating agent will be considered to be a member of the "prosecution team" will be analyzed on a case by case basis. *See* United States v. Meros, 866 F.2d 1304, 1309 (11th Cir. 1989). Not all government investigators will be considered agents of the prosecutor for *Brady* purposes, if for example they work for a different sovereign (e.g., state v. federal) or have no direct involvement in the investigation of the crime under indictment. *See* United States v. Antone, 603 F.2d 566, 569 (5th Cir. 1979).

on the prosecutor to learn of any exculpatory evidence in the possession of the police or any civilian investigators "acting on the government's behalf."[38] In contrast, ABA Model Rule 3.8(d) requires disclosure only of evidence or information "known to prosecutor"—it does not create an affirmative duty on the part of prosecutors to seek out exculpatory information in the hands of the police.[39] This does not mean that prosecutors may turn a blind eye towards possible exculpatory evidence in the possession of the police: first, by doing so they risk running afoul of the due process clause if evidence later discovered is determined to be material; second, they would not be fulfilling their obligations as "ministers of justice" if they continued a prosecution without exploring the possibility that the police possessed information that tended to exonerate the accused. An ostrich-like approach to exculpatory evidence would waste the resources of the court system in prosecuting a potentially innocent person, and potentially allow a guilty but uncharged individual to go free. For these reasons, the ABA Criminal Justice Standards state that prosecutors should not "intentionally avoid pursuit of evidence because he or she believes it will damage the prosecution's case or aid the accused."[40] A small number of jurisdictions have incorporated this aspirational standard as an ethical mandate in their version of Rule 3.8.[41]

Another notable difference between the two disclosure standards is that ABA Model Rule 3.8(d) contains no explicit reference to "impeachment" material. While the Supreme Court's decision in *United States v. Bagley*[42] requires disclosure of evidence that can be used to impeach government witnesses provided that it is "material," the "tends to negate guilt" standard of Rule 3.8(d) is silent with respect to a prosecutor's obligations in this area. Some impeaching evidence clearly comes within the ethical mandate; for exam-

38. Kyles v. Whitley, 514 U.S. 419, 437 (1995).

39. *See* Stanley Z. Fisher, *The Prosecutor's Ethical Duty to Seek Exculpatory Evidence in Police Hands: Lessons from England*, 68 FORDHAM. L. REV. 1379, 1423–24 (2000) (recommending amendment to Rule 3.8 to require prosecutors to make "reasonable efforts" to insure that police officers disclose to prosecutors evidence that tends to negate the guilt of the accused).

40. ABA Criminal Justice Standard 3–3.11(c).

41. *See, e.g.,* D.C. R. Prof'l Conduct 3.8(d); Mass. R. Prof'l Conduct 3.8(j).

42. 473 U.S. 667 (1985).

ple, if an eyewitness to a crime previously gave a statement to the police indicating that the defendant was *not* the perpetrator, and later had a change of heart and identified the accused, the prior inconsistent statement is both impeachment information (that is, it could be used to show lack of credibility) and factually exculpatory (that is, it would "tend to negate" the defendant's guilt if the jury believed the witness's first version of events). Other forms of impeachment material, however, are not so central to the defendant's guilt or innocence that they would be considered to have a "tendency to negate guilt" (e.g., inconsistencies over time in minor or collateral details of a witness's version of events). The Ethics 2000 Commission, appointed by the American Bar Association to study and recommend reform of the Model Rules, initially proposed a revised comment to Model Rule 3.8 which would have included within the scope of mandated disclosure "evidence which materially tends to impeach a government witness."[43] After receiving input from a variety of sources objecting to the indefiniteness of this phrase, the Commission decided against "attempting to explicate the relationship between paragraph (d) of this Rule and the prosecutor's constitutional obligations under *Brady* and its progeny," in the end deleting the proposed comment to Rule 3.8(d).[44]

Another important difference between the constitutional disclosure obligation and the rules of professional conduct is that *Brady* requires disclosure of exculpatory "evidence," whereas Rule 3.8(d) requires disclosure of all exculpatory "evidence or information." What is the difference between "evidence" and "information?" The word "evidence" suggests that the material would be admissible in court. The word "information" suggests a broader obligation to disclose material that would be useful in preparing a defense, even if it is not directly admissible. For example, the police may receive an anonymous tip that someone other than the accused committed the crime. Anonymous tips are hearsay,

43. *See* ABA Ethics 2000 Commission, *Proposed Rule 3.8—Public Discussion Draft,* comment [4] (April 13, 2000, on file with the American Bar Association Center for Professional Responsibility).

44. *See* Margaret Colgate Love, *The Revised ABA Model Rules of Professional Conduct: Summary of the Work of Ethics 2000,* 15 GEO. J. LEGAL ETHICS 441, 469 (2002).

and are unlikely to be admissible in court. However, they are clearly useful to the defendant, because they could lead to the production of admissible evidence if the defendant were able to track down the anonymous source, or were allowed to cross examine a police witness regarding the choices the officer made in pursuing some avenues of investigation and not others. While the ethical rules of most jurisdictions would require disclosure of such information, the issue is far from resolved under the due process clause. In *Wood v. Bartholomew*,[45] the Supreme Court found no due process violation where the prosecutor failed to reveal that one of its witnesses had failed a pre-trial polygraph examination. The Court stated that there was no *Brady* violation in that case, because polygraph tests (inadmissible under the law of the pertinent jurisdiction) were "not 'evidence' at all."[46] Moreover, the court noted that the claim that this information was materially exculpatory within the meaning of *Brady* was based on "mere speculation;"[47] even if the information might have led to some admissible evidence, there was no reasonable probability that the result at trial would have been different in light of the strength of the government's evidence in that case. The federal circuit courts are presently split on whether *Wood* excludes nonevidentiary "information" from the scope of the *Brady* disclosure obligation altogether, or merely stands for the narrower proposition that there must be some proof that the withheld "information" would have led to the introduction of exculpatory evidence that could have materially aided the defendant's case.[48]

Other sorts of "information" are not exculpatory either within the *Brady* line of cases or the ethical rule. For example, the unavailability of witnesses, the unanticipated delay in completion of scientific tests, and the prosecutor's lack of preparation for trial would surely be helpful pieces of information for the defendant to know in mounting his defense or deciding whether to plead guilty; nonetheless,

45. 516 U.S. 1 (1995).

46. *Id.* at 6.

47. *Id.*

48. *See* Gregory S. Seador, Note, *Searching for the Truth or a Game of Strategy? The Circuit Split Over the Prosecution's Obligation to Disclose Inadmissible Exculpatory Information to the Accused*, 51 SYRACUSE L. REV. 139 (2001).

these matters are surely not "evidence" within the meaning of *Brady,* and are also not information that tends to "negate" the defendant's factual guilt within the meaning of Model Rule 3.8(d). Some courts have ruled, for example, that a prosecutor has no obligation to disclose to the defendant that an important eyewitness has died before allowing the defendant to accept a guilty plea to the offense charged.[49]

Neither the due process clause nor Rule 3.8 require a prosecutor to disclose the entire contents of their file to the defendant.[50] There may be matters that a prosecutor, as a guardian of the public interest, has a critical duty to safeguard, such as information that would jeopardize the completion of another ongoing criminal investigation, information that could compromise the safety of a confidential informant, or mental impressions/work-product of the lawyer himself. Nevertheless, *doubtful* cases should always be resolved in favor of disclosure.[51] Society's interest in obtaining a verdict worthy of confidence (whether it is a conviction or an acquittal) requires a fair playing field that can only be achieved through full disclosure to the defendant of pertinent facts. Moreover, nondisclosure of evidence risks tying up the criminal justice system in post-trial motions and potential re-trials should the undisclosed information later come to light. A prosecutor in doubt about his disclosure obligations in sensitive or difficult cases may seek guidance from the court by disclosing the material to the judge *in camera,* and allowing the court to rule on whether it should be provided to the defendant.[52]

PROBLEMS

1. Assistant District Attorney William Gottlieb is prosecuting a charge of armed robbery. The police report reveals that a hooded gunman robbed a convenience store near closing time. The cashier sounded a silent alarm, and the responding officers captured the defendant blocks from the site of the robbery. According to the police report, the cashier and two customers in the store at

49. *See* People v. Jones, 44 N.Y.2d 76, 404 N.Y.S.2d 85, 375 N.E.2d 41, 44–45 (1978).

50. *Kyles* 514 U.S. at 437.

51. *Id.* at 439.

52. Under ABA Model Rule 3.8(d), a prosecutor's disclosure responsibilities under the rule may be relieved "by a protective order of the tribunal."

the time of the hold-up were shown photo arrays of potential suspects on the day after the defendant's arrest, and each picked out the defendant as the perpetrator.

While interviewing the arresting officer in preparation for trial, the prosecutor learns that the policeman interviewed a third customer in the convenience store the day after the robbery who is not mentioned anywhere in the police report. This witness gave a description of the assailant similar to the one provided by the cashier and the other two customers, but was *unable* to pick out the perpetrator from an array of photographs which included a photograph of the defendant. According to the police officer, he did not include this witness's information in his police report, "because he didn't think it was important given the strength of the other identifications." Should the prosecutor disclose the identity of this customer and the results of the identification procedure to counsel for the defendant?

2. Assistant District Attorney Edward Rapacki is assigned to prosecute a case involving indecent assault and battery on three teenaged girls. The investigation revealed that a guidance counselor at a local high school kissed and fondled three female students in his charge. The report of the investigating officer reveals that the most recent incident of battery occurred six years and two months prior to the issuance of the complaint. The statute of limitations for indecent assault and battery on a minor in the jurisdiction is presently ten years, but the statute was amended only one year ago, and provided at the time of the alleged offense a six year period of limitations.

a. The prosecutor researches the law and discovers that the defense may have a colorable motion to dismiss the case. Must the prosecutor reveal the statute of limitations defense to opposing counsel?

b. On the date scheduled for trial, the prosecutor learns that one of the three victims recently died in an automobile accident. Counsel for the defendant has indicated that his client is considering entering a guilty plea on all three counts. Must the prosecutor disclose the victim's death to defense counsel?

3. Assistant District Attorney Maria Gomez is prosecuting a charge of trafficking in cocaine. According to the police report, an informant introduced an undercover police officer to an individual capable of supplying large amounts of cocaine. Upon delivering one kilogram of cocaine to the police officer, the suspect was arrested. A subsequent search of the defendant's apartment pur-

suant to a warrant uncovered drug paraphernalia and over $50,000 in cash, which were seized.

The drug deal occurred in such a manner that the informant was a percipient witness to the hand-to-hand sale. The court orders the prosecutor to reveal the informant's identity to the accused. The police had agreed with the informant, prior to the drug deal, that they would pay him up to 10% of any assets forfeited in the case. Is this agreement exculpatory evidence which must be disclosed to the defense? Must the prosecutor disclose it only if she intends to call the informant as a witness in her case in chief?

CHAPTER SIX

PLEA BARGAINING

Many of the ethical rules directed at prosecutors assume an adversarial system where a neutral factfinder will determine the guilt or innocence of the accused. Toward that end, prosecutors are admonished to make disclosure of exculpatory evidence to the defendant, and to take other steps to insure a fair trial. Yet the reality is that well over ninety percent of criminal cases are resolved not by trial, but by guilty plea.[1] In the vast majority of cases brought in state and federal court, criminal defendants agree to waive their rights to trial and to plead guilty in exchange for charging or sentencing concessions by the prosecutor. The Supreme Court has called plea bargaining both an "important"[2] and an "essential"[3] component of our criminal justice system.

The popularity of plea bargaining stems from the advantages both sides gain by resolving criminal matters short of trial. The government avoids the uncertainties of litigation. Where a plea bargain is entered, the government assures that some punishment is meted out to the defendant, which may satisfy the public's interest in supervision of a dangerous individual. Moreover, the government avoids having to call the victims and other witnesses to the stand; embarrassment, fear, and privacy concerns of government witnesses can all be powerful inducements to "settle" a criminal case. Finally, plea bargaining conserves the resources of prosecutors, police, and the courts, which is consistent with a

1. *See* George Fisher, PLEA BARGAINING'S TRIUMPH: A HISTORY OF PLEA BARGAINING IN AMERICA, 233 Tbl. 9.1 (Stanford Univ. Press 2003).

2. Bordenkircher v. Hayes, 434 U.S. 357, 361 (1978).

3. Santobello v. New York, 404 U.S. 257, 260 (1971).

prosecutor's obligation to be mindful of the proper administration of justice across the system.

The defendant also enjoys advantages from plea bargaining that he would not enjoy at trial; including the prompt resolution of the charges against him, the reduction of risk, and an agreement by the prosecutor to lower the defendant's exposure to punishment by reducing the charges or recommending a lenient sentence. Even under a "sentencing guideline" system, where the defendant's ultimate sentence is fixed by a predetermined range, the prosecutor has the power to offer concessions to the defendant in order to induce him to plead guilty, including agreeing to stipulate about the presence or absence of certain facts that might be considered aggravating or mitigating under the guidelines, and the power to represent to the court that the defendant has cooperated substantially with the government.

Notwithstanding these mutual advantages, plea bargains are *not* transactions between equals. In most situations, the prosecutor wields power vastly greater than the defendant in plea negotiations due to his control over access to witnesses and information, and his ability through the selection of charges to dictate the maximum exposure that the defendant will face. Due to this inequality of bargaining power, a prosecutor should not assume that merely because the defendant accepts his terms and decides to plead guilty, that the end result is necessarily "just." There are several reasons why even an *innocent* defendant might accept a reduced sentence and plead guilty, especially if he has a substantial criminal record and is facing a lengthy sentence. For example, an innocent defendant may plead guilty to protect other people involved in the crime; to spare loved ones the expense and embarrassment of trial, to avoid an unduly harsh mandatory sentence, or to avoid the risk that defense counsel will perform ineffectively on his behalf.

A prosecutor's obligation to act as a "minister of justice"[4] applies as much to bargained-for outcomes as to judicially determined ones. The prosecutor must ensure that there is a sound factual predicate to the charges the defendant is willing to plead guilty to, that the negotiated sen-

4. ABA Model Rule 3.8, Comment
[1].

tence is consistent with the needs of public safety and deterrence, and that the bargained-for result is not dissimilar to outcomes achieved in other similar cases.

A. Due Process Limitations

A guilty plea provoked by coercion will be considered involuntary and in violation of due process. In *Brady v. United States*[5] the Supreme Court stated that "the agents of the state many not produce a plea by actual or threatened physical harm or by mental coercion overbearing the will of the defendant." Torture, threats of physical harm to the defendant, his family or loved ones, or playing upon the mental anxieties or fears of the accused may all be considered sufficient to deprive the accused of his freedom of choice.[6]

The Supreme Court held in *Bordenkircher v. Hayes*[7] that due process is not offended where a prosecutor threatens to indict the defendant on greater charges if he rejects a plea bargain and elects to proceed to trial. Given the "mutuality of advantage" flowing to both parties in the plea bargaining context, the Court refused to equate the "give and take" of plea bargaining with vindictive prosecution under its earlier due process rulings in *Blackledge v. Perry*[8] and *North Carolina v. Pearce.*[9]

> While confronting a defendant with the risk of more severe punishment clearly may have a "discouraging effect on the defendant's assertion of his trial rights, the imposition of these difficult choices [is] an inevitable"— and permissible—"attribute of any legitimate system which tolerates and encourages the negotiation of pleas."[10]

5. 397 U.S. 742, 750 (1970) (defendant's guilty plea not rendered involuntary by fear of death penalty).

6. People v. Picciotti, 4 N.Y.2d 340, 175 N.Y.S.2d 32, 151 N.E.2d 191, 194 (1958). *See* State v. Wilson, 31 S.W.3d 189, 195 (Tenn. 2000).

7. 434 U.S. 357, 363 (1978).

8. 417 U.S. 21 (1974) (re-indicting defendant on more serious charges af-ter filing of appeal creates a presumption of vindictiveness).

9. 395 U.S. 711 (1969) (sentencing defendant to greater term of imprisonment after successful appeal creates a presumption of vindictiveness).

10. *Bordenkircher*, 434 U.S. at 364, quotation omitted.

Under *Bordenkircher*, so long as the government is acting in good faith and without discriminatory motive, it does not offend due process principles for the prosecutor to place time limits on the acceptance or rejection of a plea offer; for the prosecutor to condition a plea offer on the defendant's withdrawal of a motion to suppress or dismiss; for a prosecutor to re-indict the defendant on new or more serious charges after the defendant has elected to reject a plea offer and proceed to trial; or, for the prosecutor to recommend a greater sentence following trial than he recommended during plea discussions.

The Supreme Court has looked to contract principles to determine the validity and enforceability of plea bargains between a prosecutor and a criminal defendant. In *Santobello v. New York*,[11] the defendant entered into a plea arrangement with the prosecutor agreeing to plead guilty to a lesser included offense in exchange for the prosecutor's agreement to make no specific sentencing recommendation to the court. The defendant's guilty plea was accepted by the court, but substantial time passed before the imposition of sentence. At the time of sentencing, a new prosecutor was assigned to the case. The new prosecutor recommended that the defendant receive the statutory maximum one year in prison, and the court imposed that sentence. The Supreme Court ruled that the defendant was entitled to relief:

> [W]hen a plea rests in any significant degree on a promise or agreement of the prosecutor, so that it can be said to be part of the inducement or consideration, such promise must be fulfilled.

The Court in *Santobello* remanded for consideration of the appropriate remedy in the case, noting that where the prosecutor has failed to live up to any promises under a plea agreement, the court may either 1) require specific performance of the government's side of the bargain, or 2) allow the defendant to withdraw his guilty plea and proceed to trial.[12]

One lesson of *Santobello* is that prosecutors should keep a record in their files of any plea offers made to defense

---

11. 404 U.S. 257 (1971).

12. *Id.* at 263. For examples of cases taking each approach, *see* United States v. Palladino, 347 F.3d 29, 35 (2nd Cir. 2003) (withdrawal of plea); Buckley v. Terhune, 266 F.Supp.2d 1124, 1143 (C.D. Cal. 2002) (specific performance).

counsel. This is especially important in a busy state district court where a case may be passed between staff assistants at various stages of the proceedings. As the Court noted in *Santobello,* "[t]he staff lawyers in a prosecutor's office have the burden of 'letting the left hand know what the right hand is doing.'"[13] The Court ruled that even agreements made by *other* prosecutors within the same office could be judicially enforced, provided that the government's offer was accepted by the defendant and supported by consideration. Consideration will be found where the defendant performs some obligation under the agreement (such as by providing information to investigators) or relies upon the agreement to his detriment (such as by pleading guilty).

Where a prosecutor enters into a plea agreement with one defendant among a group of codefendants alleged to be joint venturers in criminal activity, it is improper for the prosecutor to make a plea offer conditional on the defendant's refusal to testify in favor of accomplices.[14] A prosecutor justifiably might be concerned that once a defendant has "pled out" and reaped the benefit of a favorable deal, he will attempt to assist co-defendants by testifying falsely at their upcoming trial. Appropriate ways to minimize this risk include delaying the defendant's change of plea until after the trial of co-defendants, or engaging in a detailed factual plea colloquy that locks the defendant in, under oath, to a particular version of events.[15] The threat of a perjury prosecution or recision of the deal may be adequate deterrents to a "turncoat" accomplice. However, as discussed in Chapter 4, it violates due process to impede a defendant's access to witnesses by instructing them not to testify in favor of co-defendants, or by penalizing them for testifying truthfully.

It is not impermissible under the due process clause for a prosecutor to leverage a guilty plea by threatening the defendant with the prosecution of another person (such as a family member or loved one). So long as the prosecutor is acting in good faith and has probable cause to believe that the third party is involved in criminal activity, courts have

---

13. *Id.* at 262.
14. United States v. Bell, 506 F.2d 207, 222 (D.C. Cir. 1974).

15. Cassidy, *supra* ch. 5 n.12, at 1145–46.

found such third party beneficiary agreements acceptable.[16] However, because a guilty plea made in consideration of lenient treatment towards third parties poses a "greater danger of coercion" than purely bilateral agreements, courts have scrutinized these agreements carefully to make sure that the prosecutor acted in good faith in characterizing the potential exposure of the third party, and that the defendant entered his guilty plea voluntarily.[17]

It is not unconstitutionally coercive for a prosecutor to condition a plea offer to a defendant on the willingness of other defendants in the same transaction to also plead guilty. So-called "packaged" or "wired" plea agreements— where the prosecutor's offer of leniency to one defendant is conditioned on the acceptance of plea concessions made to others—have been upheld as permissible so long as they are entered into by the codefendants knowingly and intelligently.[18] A prosecutor may find it advantageous to enter into a "packaged" plea arrangement where the benefits to be obtained from a guilty plea against one defendant are outweighed by the costs associated with having to proceed to trial against others, in the absence of a full resolution of all the cases. This is consistent with a prosecutor's responsibility to consider the proper allocation of law enforcement resources in enforcing the criminal laws.

How much discovery must a prosecutor turn over to the accused before the defendant enters a guilty plea? The obligation to disclose exculpatory evidence under *Brady v. Maryland* was implemented to avoid "unfair trial[s]"[19] Discovery of *Brady* material is thus a *trial* right; by the express terms of the decision, the constitutional obligation has no application where the defendant elects to waive a trial and plead guilty. However, discovering weaknesses in the prosecutor's case would certainly assist the defendant in accurately assessing the likelihood of conviction following trial, which is essential to a fully informed plea negotiation. For this

16. *See, e.g.,* United States v. Arrellano, 213 F.3d 427, 431 (8th Cir. 2000); United States v. McBride, 571 F.Supp. 596, 615 (S.D. Tex. 1983).

17. *See* United States v. Nuckols, 606 F.2d 566, 569 (5th Cir. 1979).

18. *See, e.g.,* United States v. Armas, 11 Fed. Appx. 899, 900, 2001 WL 409033 (9th Cir. 2001); United States v. Vest, 125 F.3d 676, 679 (8th Cir. 1997).

19. 373 U.S. at 87.

reason, many commentators have argued that prosecutors should turn over *Brady* material prior to a guilty plea.[20] However, state and federal courts are divided on this important question; that is, whether a defendant who chooses to plead guilty can claim the protections of *Brady* where favorable information in the possession of the government comes to light following the imposition of sentence.[21]

In *United States v. Ruiz*,[22] the Supreme Court resolved this controversy for federal prosecutors, at least in part. The Court ruled that the Due Process Clause of the Fifth Amendment does not require federal prosecutors to disclose impeachment information or information supporting affirmative defenses prior to a guilty plea.

> [T]he Constitution . . . does not require complete knowledge of the relevant circumstances, but permits a court to accept a guilty plea, with its accompanying waiver of various constitutional rights, despite various forms of misapprehension under which a defendant might labor.[23]

The Court in *Ruiz* left unaddressed the question of whether due process principles might be offended where the prosecutor withholds information prior to a guilty plea that supports the *factual innocence* of the accused, or requires the defendant to explicitly waive his right to such material as a condition of a plea bargain. The proposed agreement at issue in *Ruiz* obligated the prosecutor to disclose this narrow class of highly exculpatory *Brady* material prior to the change of plea.[24]

Notwithstanding this open issue,[25] prosecutors would be well advised to disclose to the defendant any information that supports the factual innocence of the accused prior to a change of plea (such as exculpatory test results, or statements from witnesses that indicate another person committed the crime). This is advisable not only to prevent the possible punishment of an innocent person, but also to conserve prosecutorial and judicial resources. A defendant

---

20. *See, e.g.,* Corrina Barrett Lain, *Accuracy Where it Matters: Brady v. Maryland in the Plea Bargaining Context*, 80 Wash U. L. Q. 1 (2002).

21. *Id.* at 6.

22. 536 U.S. 622 (2002).

23. *Id.* at 630 (citations omitted).

24. *See id.* at 631.

25. *See* McCann v. Mangialardi, 337 F.3d 782, 787 (7th Cir. 2003).

who learns of exonerating information after his sentence is imposed may seek to withdraw his plea on the constitutional ground that it was not intelligently and voluntarily entered,[26] or on the state statutory ground that the conviction was based on a "manifest injustice."[27] In these circumstances, the resources of the prosecutor and the courts will be tied up in litigating a motion for new trial that could have been avoided by an appropriate and timely disclosure. Moreover, as discussed in Chapter 5, the ethical rule pertaining to disclosure of exculpatory evidence requires prosecutors to hand over discovery in a "timely" manner,[28] without regards to whether the criminal matter is resolved by a trial or a change of plea.

B. Ethical Considerations

Given that the overwhelming majority of criminal cases are resolved by plea bargains, it is surprising that Codes of Professional Conduct in effect in most states provide little guidance for prosecutors in this area. In fact, ABA Model Rule 3.8, entitled "Special Responsibilities of a Prosecutor," contains no express reference whatsoever to negotiations or plea bargaining.

Two ABA-recommended disciplinary rules that arguably constrain a prosecutor's conduct during plea bargaining are 1) the prohibition on "conduct involving dishonesty, fraud, deceit or misrepresentation" contained in ABA Model Rule 8.4, and 2) the prohibition of "false statement of fact or law to a tribunal" contained in ABA Model Rule 3.3(a)(1). A prosecutor who misrepresents to defense counsel the facts of the case or the availability of a witness in order to induce a guilty plea violates Rule 8.4. Bravado by the prosecutor concerning the government's chances of success following trial may be tolerated, but only insofar as it involves personal opinion about the strength of the case and not actual misstatements of fact. A prosecutor will run afoul of the "Candor to the Tribunal" provisions of Rule 3.3 where he

26. *See* Tollett v. Henderson, 411 U.S. 258, 267 (1973) (while defendant could not raise claim of constitutional error in grand jury after guilty plea, court could entertain question of whether the guilty plea was intelli-gently and voluntarily made with the advice of competent counsel).

27. Lain, *supra* ch. 6 n.20 , at 18.

28. ABA Model Rule 3.8(d).

makes false or misleading statements to the court about the nature of the crime in an effort to either minimize or maximize the defendant's sentence (e.g., date or location of the crime, the age of the victim, the amount of contraband, or the defendant's prior record).[29]

It is improper to engage in post-charging plea discussions with a defendant before he has had the opportunity to engage counsel. Due to the inequality of power and experience between lawyers and non-lawyers, a prosecutor typically has the upper hand in negotiations with an accused. ABA Criminal Justice Standard 3–4.1 requires prosecutors to negotiate only with counsel, unless the defendant has waived counsel following arraignment and has elected to proceed *pro se*. This standard may be viewed as a specific application of ABA Model Rule 3.8(c), which prohibits a prosecutor from seeking to obtain from an unrepresented defendant a waiver of important pretrial rights. In situations where a prosecutor is negotiating with an accused representing himself, ABA Standard 3–4.1 suggests that "where feasible" a record should be made of any plea discussions. This standard can be satisfied by having an investigative officer present and taking notes when the prosecutor meets with a *pro se* defendant to discuss a change of plea. This may not always be practical in a busy community court where an accused proceeding *pro se* is charged with a misdemeanor, and approaches the prosecutor during a break in the court proceedings seeking to discuss the resolution of his case.

In exercising discretion whether to grant charging or sentencing concessions to a defendant, the prosecutor must consider a number of factors relating to the public's interest. For example, the U.S. Attorney's Manual sets forth the following list of "considerations to be weighed" in determining whether it would be appropriate to enter into a plea bargain:

   1) the defendant's willingness to cooperate in the investigation or prosecution of others;

   2) the defendant's criminal record;

---

29. U.S. Attorney's Manual 9–27.430 provides that "If a prosecutor wishes to support a departure from the guidelines, he or she should candidly do so and should not stipulate to facts that are untrue."

3) the nature and seriousness of the offense;

4) the defendant's remorse and willingness to assume responsibility;

5) the benefits to be gained from a prompt resolution of the case;

6) the likelihood of conviction following trial;

7) the likely effect on witnesses from a trial;

8) the probable sentence or other consequences;

9) the public interest in having the case tried rather than disposed of by plea;

10) the expense of trial and appeal;

11) the need to avoid delay; and

12) the effect upon the victim's right to restitution.[30]

The National District Attorneys Association recommends consideration of similar factors; however, their relevant standard regarding plea bargaining also includes reference to the "age" and "background" of the defendant and the "possible deterrent value of prosecution."[31] This latter factor suggests that in certain circumstances it may be appropriate for a prosecutor to withhold plea concessions in order to force a trial, due to the deterrent value of educating the public about the crime and its consequences.

Given the breadth and elasticity of these discretionary factors, perhaps the hardest task a prosecutor faces is to treat similarly situated defendants similarly in the plea bargaining process. As a "minister of justice," the prosecutor must strive to insure equity among defendants charged with similar offenses across time. The prosecutor should not offer the accused a "sweetheart deal" unavailable to other defendants simply because the prosecutor may be friendly with defense counsel, may be feeling tired or lazy that particular day, may wish to avoid trial before a notoriously difficult judge, or may identify with some aspect of the defendant's personal background. Recognizing the vast discretion afforded to prosecutors in the plea bargaining process, and the need to avoid disparate treatment due to

30. U.S. Attorney's Manual § 9–27.420   **31.** *See* NDAA Standard 68.1.

personal bias or prejudice, NDAA Standard 66.3 suggest that "[s]imilarly situated defendants should be afforded substantially equal plea agreement opportunities." This does not mean that all codefendants charged as joint participants in criminal activity must be afforded the same plea offer; so long as there are differences between their degree of involvement in the offense or their criminal backgrounds, differentiating between codefendants in terms of their level of dangerousness is an important part of the prosecutor's role.

PROBLEMS

1. Assistant District Attorney Mary Downing is assigned to prosecute a young woman who allegedly murdered a five-month-old infant in her care. The cause of death was shaken baby syndrome. The government possesses evidence that the nineteen-year-old defendant, who was acting as a nanny in the household of the victim, became angered at the baby's fussiness and vigorously shook the baby. The baby died five days later from massive brain injuries.

Assume that first degree murder is defined in the relevant jurisdiction as an unlawful killing with malice, committed either with deliberate premeditation or with extreme atrocity or cruelty. Second degree murder is defined as an unlawful killing with malice but *without* either deliberate premeditation or extreme atrocity of cruelty. ("Malice" is defined in the jurisdiction, for purposes of both first and second degree murder, to include "conduct which a reasonable person in the actor's situation would have known created a plain and strong likelihood of death.") Involuntary manslaughter is defined as an unintentional killing resulting from an intentional battery.

Assume that first degree murder is punishable in the jurisdiction by life in prison, without possibility of parole. Second degree murder carries a sentence of life in prison, with the possibility of parole after twenty years. Involuntary manslaughter carries an indeterminate sentence of up to fifteen years in prison, at the discretion of the judge.

> a) Is it permissible for the prosecutor to recommend to the grand jury that the defendant be indicted for first degree murder, when the prosecutor knows that she would accept a plea to manslaughter prior to trial?

> b) Assume that the grand jury indicts the defendant on a charge of first degree murder. The prosecutor informs defense

counsel following arraignment that she would accept a guilty plea to the lesser included offense of manslaughter and recommend a fifteen year sentence. Defense counsel tells the prosecutor that she will talk to her client and "get back to her." That evening, the prosecutor notifies her supervisor at the District Attorney's office of her conversation with defense counsel, and the supervisor becomes extremely upset. The supervisor states unequivocally that "under no condition will this the office accept a plea to anything less than second degree murder." Is it permissible for the prosecutor to call the defense counsel the following day and withdraw the plea offer?

2. Prosecutor William White is handling a case alleging statutory rape. The defendant is a nineteen-year-old high school senior. The victim is a fifteen-year-old high school freshman. The defendant and victim allegedly met at a house party, consumed alcoholic beverages to excess, and had consensual sex in the downstairs bedroom of the host's home. The victim suffered no physical injuries. The rape was reported to the police the day following the incident by the victim's mother, after the victim confided to her mother the events of the previous evening. The maximum sentence in the jurisdiction for statutory rape is five years in prison.

Defendant offers to admit to the facts in the criminal complaint in exchange for an agreed recommendation of pre-trial probation, community service, and dismissal of the criminal charges at the end of the probationary period. Which of the following factors—if any—should the prosecutor take into account in deciding whether to enter into this plea agreement?

a.   the victim's hesitancy to testify at trial?

b.   the victim's parent's interests in securing a conviction and jail sentence?

c.   the likelihood of conviction after trial?

d.   the likely sentence the judge assigned to the case would impose following a conviction?

e.   the government's sentencing recommendation on similar statutory rape cases recently handled by the office?

f.   the defendant's criminal history, or lack thereof?

g.   the likely impact of a criminal conviction and sentence on the defendant's plans to attend college in the coming year?

h.   the prosecutor's caseload?

    i. public sentiment, reported in the local media, reflecting outrage at the prosecution of "such a fine young man?"

3. Assistant District Attorney Howard Brick is prosecuting three youths accused of beating a male prostitute to death in the red light district of the city. All three youths are charged with murder and civil rights violations. The prosecutor has evidence that all three defendants left a nearby bar together on the night of the murder, and that they were heard on the streets shouting obscenities regarding homosexuals, and that they were seen as a group standing over the victim in the street. Forensic and eyewitness evidence links all three defendants to the scene, but who instigated the brutal crime and who played what role is in dispute. One of the defendants offers to cooperate with the government and testify at trial against his co-defendants in exchange for leniency. He will not cooperate without assurances of a suspended sentence on the civil rights charge and a dismissal of the murder count. He insists that his role was minimal compared to the others—that he cheered his friends on, and on one occasion punched the victim. What factors should the prosecutor consider in determining whether to enter into a cooperation agreement with this defendant?

CHAPTER SEVEN

TRIAL CONDUCT

A novice prosecutor might suspect that ethical vigilance is less important in the courtroom—where the judge and jury are present to mediate between opposing forces in an adversarial process. But the duty of the prosecutor to ensure a level playing field and to protect the defendant's right to a fair trial give rise to a host of ethical responsibilities in the trial setting. As the Supreme Court has observed:

> [The government lawyer] may prosecute with earnestness and vigor—indeed, he should do so. But, while he many strike hard blows, he is not at liberty to strike foul ones. It is as much his duty to refrain from improper methods calculated to produce a wrongful conviction as it is to use every legitimate means to bring about a just one.[1]

Prosecutorial overreaching at trial not only risks conviction of a factually or legally innocent person, it also risks tying up valuable public resources in post conviction proceedings that challenge the validity of the verdict. Various prohibitions of misconduct by prosecutors during trial will be discussed in this chapter. These prohibitions are rooted not only in ethical rules and standards, but also in the defendant's constitutional rights to due process,[2] to trial by jury,[3] to the assistance of counsel,[4] and to be protected from compulsory self incrimination.[5]

1. Berger v. United States, 295 U.S. 78, 88 (1935).
2. U.S. Const., Amendment V, XIV.
3. U.S. Const., Amendment VI.
4. Id.
5. U.S. Const., Amendment V.

A. Selecting and Communicating with the Jury

In jurisdictions that permit attorneys to exercise peremptory challenges during jury selection, the prosecutor must refrain from excusing members of the jury venire on the basis of their race, sex or national origin. The Supreme Court ruled in *Batson v. Kentucky* that discrimination in jury selection offends the Equal Protection Clause of the Fourteenth Amendment.[6] *Batson* established a three-stage analysis for reviewing claims of discrimination in jury selection. Where a defendant makes an adequate threshold showing that the prosecutor has engaged in a "pattern"[7] of eliminating prospective jurors on the basis of an impermissible characteristic, the judge should ask the prosecutor to state his reasons for the challenge at side bar. At this stage, the prosecutor must state a genuine, race-neutral (or sex-neutral, or national origin-neutral) reason for excluding the juror. If the prosecutor is able to do so, the court must allow the exclusion of the juror, unless the court determines at stage three of the inquiry that the reason proffered by the prosecutor is a pretext for discrimination.[8] A court may find such pretext based on an assessment of the prosecutor's demeanor and credibility, or based on its determination that other prospective jurors sharing similar articulated charac-

---

6. 476 U.S. 79 (1986). Because discrimination in jury selection effects the rights of the excluded jurors to participate in government, the court ruled in *Georgia v. McCollum*, 505 U.S. 42 (1992) that the Fourteenth Amendment prohibits discrimination by defense counsel as well the prosecutor.

7. State and federal courts have taken differing approaches on the issue of what constitutes a "pattern" of discrimination within the meaning of *Batson*. For example, challenging two jurors sharing the same race, sex or national origin out of a potential pool of three or more such jurors may constitute a pattern. *See, e.g., United States v. Omoruyi*, 7 F.3d 880, 881 (9th Cir. 1993). Striking the sole juror of a particular sex, race, or nation of origin might also be sufficient to trigger a prima facie case. *See Commonwealth v. Curtiss*, 424 Mass. 78, 676 N.E.2d 431, 434 (1997). But where there is more than one prospective juror in the pool sharing the racial sexual or national origin characteristic of the excused juror, challenging the *first* member of the venire fitting that characteristic will not without more be considered to rise to the level of a "pattern" of discrimination such that the judge can permissibly ask the prosecutor to state his reasons for the challenge. *See Batson*, 476 U.S. at 97 (court must look to totality of circumstances to determine whether defendant has made out a prima facie case of discrimination, including number of prospective jurors from that discrete group challenged and any statements made by attorney during voir dire revealing bias).

8. *Purkett v. Elem*, 514 U.S. 765, 769 (1995).

teristics but of a different race (or sex, or national origin) were not challenged by the prosecutor. To date, the Supreme Court has declined to include religion among the characteristics protected from discrimination in jury selection, although some courts applying state constitutional law have ruled that religious affiliation is an impermissible basis for excusing jurors.[9]

Ethical rules in effect in many states also prohibit discrimination in jury selection. Comment [3] to ABA Model Rule 8.4 goes beyond even constitutional constraints, providing that conduct manifesting "bias or prejudice based upon race, sex, national origin, *disability, age, sexual orientation, or socio-economic status*" constitutes conduct "prejudicial to the administration of justice."[10]

The prosecutor must avoid any private contact with jurors between the time of jury empanelment and the issuance of the jury's verdict.[11] All communications with jurors or prospective jurors must be made on the record in open court. This rule protects jurors from being improperly influenced by attorneys in the case. Sometimes juror contact can be inadvertent—such as when a prosecutor is discussing the case with a colleague on an elevator during lunch, before he realizes that a juror is present and capable of overhearing the conversation. To protect against even inadvertent juror contact, a prosecutor should avoid conversations about a pending case in public areas of the courtroom where jurors might overhear. All pre-verdict juror contact—including inadvertent contact and instances where a juror intentionally contacts the prosecutor outside the courtroom in person, by phone, or by mail—should be reported to the judge presiding over the case.

B. Opening Statements

During the opening statement, a prosecutor should not allude to any evidence unless he has a good faith basis for

9. *See* Davis v. Minnesota, 511 U.S. 1115 (1994) (denying certiorari). *See also* State v. Eason, 336 N.C. 730, 445 S.E.2d 917 (1994).

10. Comment [3] to ABA Model Rule 8.4 goes on to state that a judge's finding that "peremptory challenges were exercised on a discriminatory basis does not *alone* establish a violation of this rule" (emphasis supplied).

11. ABA Model Rule 3.5(b). *See also* ABA Criminal Justice Standard 3–5.4(a).

believing that this evidence will be tendered by the government and admitted by the court.[12] Reference in an opening statement to evidence of dubious admissibility runs the risk of inviting a mistrial if the judge later excludes the evidence, and a cautionary instruction to the jury is considered incapable of alleviating any resulting prejudice to the defendant. Matters the prosecutor should normally avoid mentioning in an opening statement include lay witness opinion, hearsay not fitting clearly within any exception to the hearsay rule, expert opinion about novel or unprecedented technologies, and the character or criminal record of the accused. Where the prosecutor wishes to resolve legal issues about admissibility prior to trial in order to allow himself the option of referring to the evidence during his opening statement, he should ask for a pre-trial ruling by filing a motion in limine prior to jury empanelment.

A prosecutor should not display physical exhibits to the jury during an opening statement without the advance permission of the court. ABA Criminal Justice Standard 3–5.6(c) provides that:

> A prosecutor should not permit any tangible evidence to be displayed in the view of the judge or jury which would tend to prejudice fair consideration by the judge or jury until such time as a good faith tender of such evidence is made.

The purpose of an opening statement is to explain to the jury the charges in the case and the nature of the government's proof. Unlike a closing argument, it is not necessary during the opening for a prosecutor to marshal all of the state's evidence against the accused, or to display various pieces of physical evidence that will be used to link the defendant to the crime. An oral description of the government's case is sufficient. Use of physical exhibits during an opening statement risks exposing the jury to highly inflammatory material that may later be excluded.

C.   Examination of Witnesses

During direct examination of a witness, it is improper for the prosecutor to knowingly elicit false testimony. Such

---

12. *See* ABA Model Rule 3.4(e); ABA Criminal Justice Standard 3–5.5.

conduct violates both the Rules of Professional Conduct[13] and the defendant's constitutional right to a fair trial under the due process clause.[14] If the prosecutor is aware that a witness intends to testify falsely, he must either counsel the witness against perjury, or decline to call the witness to the stand. If the prosecutor learns of the falsity of a witness's testimony during the testimony or after it is presented, and the testimony relates to a material fact, the prosecutor is ethically obligated to take "reasonable remedial measures"[15] to rectify the perjury, which may include either correcting the false testimony on redirect examination, or calling the false testimony to the attention of the court and defense counsel at sidebar.[16] The prosecutor's duty to correct false testimony continues past trial and through the duration of the "proceedings;" that is, until an appeal has been decided or the time for filing a notice of appeal has passed.[17]

During cross examination, a prosecutor may not ask a witness a question that assumes the truth of a factual predicate, where the prosecutor has no good faith basis for believing that fact to be true.[18] Due to the latitude afforded attorneys to ask leading questions on cross examination, this form of inquiry can be a powerful tool to implant suggestions in the jurors' minds that may not be supported by admissible evidence. For example, if the prosecutor asks an alibi witness the question "Isn't it true that you were fired from your last job for stealing company property?," even if the witness answers "no" to this question the insinuation may leave an indelible mark on the jury. The tactic of asking questions on cross examination without any factual foundation might violate the defendant's constitutional right to a fair trial, if the information suggested by the prosecutor is materially damaging to the defendant and not supportable

13. ABA Model Rule 3.3(a)(3).

14. Miller v. Pate, 386 U.S. 1, 7 (1967).

15. ABA Model Rule 3.3(a)(3).

16. The ABA Criminal Justice Standards take an even stricter approach to a prosecutor's responsibility with respect to false testimony than the Model Rules of Professional Conduct, requiring the prosecutor to "seek withdrawal [of the evidence] upon discovery of its falsity," without regard to materiality. *See* Standard 3–5.6.

17. ABA Model Rule 3.3, Comment [13].

18. ABA Criminal Justice Standard 3–5.7(d).

either by admissible evidence or the prosecutor's good faith belief that such evidence exists.[19]

A prosecutor must take great care when cross examining the accused. The prosecutor may not explicitly or implicitly comment on the defendant's silence when questioned by the police upon his arrest. The Supreme Court ruled in *Doyle v. Ohio*[20] that a defendant's due process rights are violated where a prosecutor attempts to impeach the defendant's trial testimony by asking him to explain why he did not tell a similar story to the police following his arrest and the receipt of *Miranda* warnings. Reasoning that *Miranda* contains an implicit assurance that an accused's election to remain silent will not be used against him on a future occasion, the Court based its holding largely upon the rationale that post-*Miranda* silence is state-induced, and that using such silence against a defendant on cross examination violates fundamental fairness. However, the Court has identified one important exception to the *Doyle* rule. Where the accused does *not* remain silent, but chooses instead to make a statement to the police after receiving *Miranda* warnings, the prosecutor is free to impeach the defendant if he testifies to a different version of events at trial, and can ask the defendant why he omitted certain details from the story which he earlier told to the police.[21] Since even prior inconsistent statements elicited in violation of *Miranda* may be used to impeach a defendant who testifies at trial,[22] the Court has concluded that it does not offend due process for a prosecutor to impeach an arrestee who chooses to speak with his omission of certain details in a post-arrest statement.

The constitutional limitation on impeaching a defendant with his prior silence is narrow. The Supreme Court has ruled that it does not offend due process for a prosecutor to impeach a testifying defendant with his silence *prior to arrest*, or with his silence *after arrest, and before being provided with Miranda warnings*. The Court has expressly

19. *See* Berger v. United States, 295 U.S. 78, 84 (1935). *Compare* United States v. Whitmore, 359 F.3d 609, 621 (D.C. Cir. 2004) (prosecutor only must have good faith basis to ask question) *with* Commonwealth v. Wynter, 55 Mass.App.Ct. 337, 341, 770 N.E.2d 542 (2002) (prosecutor must be pre- pared to prove impeachment with admissible evidence).

20. 426 U.S. 610, 619 (1976).

21. Anderson v. Charles, 447 U.S. 404, 409 (1980).

22. Harris v. New York, 401 U.S. 222 (1971).

distinguished these two situations from the silence post-arrest and post-*Miranda* found to be off limits in *Doyle*, reasoning that in the absence of the implied assurances contained within the *Miranda* warnings that silence will not be used against the accused, the government has not had a hand in inducing the defendant's silence. In *Jenkins v. Anderson*,[23] the Court ruled that it does not offend due process for a prosecutor to cross examine a defendant to impeach his trial testimony by asking him why he did not come forward to tell authorities his version of events between the date of the incident and his arrest. In *Fletcher v. Weir*,[24] the Court ruled that it does not offend due process for a prosecutor to impeach a defendant by asking him on cross examination why he did not tell the police his version of events between the time of his apprehension and his advisement of *Miranda* warnings later the same day at the police station. Prosecutors should be cautioned, however, that with respect to post-arrest, pre-*Miranda* silence, several state courts have declined to embrace the controversial reasoning of *Fletcher v. Weir,* either as a matter of state constitutional law[25] or state rules of evidence.[26]

A difficult issue in the field of prosecutorial ethics is whether a prosecutor may cross examine a witness to undermine his credibility where the prosecutor believes that the witness is testifying truthfully.[27] Imagine a scenario where the defendant is charged with "operating under the influence" for driving drunk late one Friday evening. Defense counsel calls the defendant's employer as a witness, who testifies 1) that the defendant was sober when he left work on the afternoon in question, and 2) that the defendant is a conscientious and reliable employee. Neither of these facts, if

23. 447 U.S. 231, 240 (1980) (impeachment of defendant's self defense claim with failure to come forward until two weeks after incident).

24. 455 U.S. 603, 607 (1982) (allowing impeachment of defendant's claim of accidental stabbing by his failure to tell police about accident immediately upon turning himself in to police station).

25. *See, e.g.,* Commonwealth v. Turner, 499 Pa. 579, 454 A.2d 537, 540

(1982); Anderson v. State, 758 S.W.2d 676, 683 (Tex. App. 1988).

26. *See, e.g.,* People v. Conyers, 52 N.Y.2d 454, 438 N.Y.S.2d 741, 420 N.E.2d 933, 934 (App. 1981) (balancing probative value against prejudicial effect); State v. Ospina, 81 Ohio App.3d 644, 611 N.E.2d 989, 993 (10th Dist. 1992) (same).

27. *See* Bruce A. Green, *Prosecutorial Ethics as Usual,* 2003 U. Ill. L. Rev. 1573, 1596 (2003).

true, directly undercuts the prosecutor's theory of his case, and the prosecutor has no reason to believe that either of these facts is false. Should the prosecutor cross examine the employer? What if the prosecutor has information that the witness has a prior criminal conviction for fraud? Or that he lied on his application for military service? The prosecutor would not be acting as a minister of "justice" if he attempted to discredit the witness in order to have the jury discount testimony that is true. In that situation, the prosecutor would be directing the jury's attention away from the truth and toward falsehood. But the prosecutor cannot really "know" the truth of any fact, unless he was there to witness it firsthand. Moreover, refraining from cross examining a witness to expose credibility problems may hamper the jury in their task of sorting out truth from falsity, and weighing the significance of facts proven to their satisfaction. The ABA Criminal Justice Standards do not answer this difficult question, although they attempt to provide some guidance. Standard 3–5.7(b) suggests that "the prosecutor's *belief* that a witness is telling the truth does not preclude cross examination," but that "a prosecutor should not use the power of cross-examination to discredit or undermine a witness if the prosecutor *knows* the witness is testifying truthfully." The standard also suggests that it is improper for a prosecutor to conduct a cross-examination solely to "intimidate or humiliate" a witness.

D. Closing Argument

A common claim on appeal of a criminal conviction is that the prosecutor's closing argument was misleading, inflammatory, or overly prejudicial. Misconduct by prosecutors in closing argument occurs with "disturbing frequency" in criminal trials, and this problem has commanded the close attention and frustration of appellate courts.[28] There are two likely explanations for why prosecutors so frequently overstep the proper bounds of summation: 1) they are caught up in the intensity of the adversarial process, and are motivated to win at all costs; and 2) they are overly prone to theatrics and dramatic spectacles at a point in the proceedings when

28. *See* United States v. Martinez–Medina, 279 F.3d 105, 127–128 (1st Cir. 2002).

they stand at the center of the jury's attention. Whatever the cause, adequate preparation, forethought, and self restraint by prosecutors can avoid many of the defects typically found in government summations. While a comprehensive review of all possible forms of prosecutorial error during closing argument is beyond the scope of this text,[29] there are six "cardinal sins" of closing argument that should be scrupulously avoided.

First, it is unethical for the prosecutor to state his personal opinion about the guilt or innocence of the defendant.[30] The jury should make their determination in the case based on their assessment of the physical evidence and the credibility of the witnesses, not their identification with or affinity towards counsel. When a prosecutor expresses his personal belief in the defendant's guilt, he is exploiting the power and trust that the jury may place in the government; the jury may improperly conclude that the prosecutor has access to extrajudicial information about which they are unaware.[31] The prohibition against expressing a personal opinion in guilt may be violated directly (e.g., "After listening to the testimony, I am fully confident that the defendant is guilty") or more subtly (e.g., "The government would not have wasted the time of this court and jury unless we were satisfied of the defendant's guilt beyond a reasonable doubt"). In order to avoid comments that could later be construed by an appellate court as stating a personal opinion about the case, the prosecutor should use terms such as "I submit" or "I suggest" when arguing appropriate inferences to be drawn from evidence, rather than the more perilous phrase "I believe."[32]

Second, it is unethical conduct for the prosecutor to assert a personal opinion about the credibility of any witness.[33] The prosecutor may argue to the jury *why* certain witnesses should be believed or disbelieved, by drawing the

29. For an excellent discussion and compendium of appellate decisions in this area, *see* Charles L. Cantrell, *Prosecutorial Misconduct: Recognizing Errors in Closing Argument*, 26 Am. J. Trial Advoc. 535 (2003).

30. ABA Model Rule 3.4(e); ABA Criminal Justice Standard 3–5.8(b).

31. United States v. Young, 470 U.S. 1, 18 (1985).

32. *Modica*, 663 F.2d at 1181.

33. ABA Model Rule 3.4(e); ABA Criminal Justice Standard 3–5.8(b).

jury's attention to their demeanor, their motivation in the case, and consistencies or inconsistencies in their testimony. In fact, closing argument is precisely the prosecutor's opportunity to do so. But the prosecutor may not ethically interpose his own credibility before the jury by suggesting that the prosecutor himself believes or disbelieves a certain witness.[34] For example, a summation would run afoul of the "no-vouching" rule if a prosecutor argued to the jury that "I found that witness to be incredibly honest" or "I would never have put that witness on the stand unless I believed him to be truthful." In this regard, the prosecutor must be particularly careful when dealing with an accomplice witness who is testifying pursuant to a cooperation agreement with the government. Where the agreement conditions certain benefits to the witness on the witness's obligation to "tell the truth," and the written agreement is placed before the jury, the prosecutor must not suggest in his closing argument that the government has any special means of ascertaining the truthfulness of the witness's testimony, or that the prosecutor would not have entered into a plea bargain with the witness if he had believed him to be fabricating his version of events.[35]

Third, it is unethical conduct for the prosecutor to argue facts not in evidence, misstate the evidence, or argue inferences not supported by the evidence.[36] "Assertions of facts not proven amount to unsworn testimony of the advocate and are not subject to cross examination. Prosecutors have aptly been condemned by courts for the clearly improper use before the jury of evidence that had not been . . . introduced at trial."[37] This prohibition may be violated where the prosecutor misquotes words uttered by a witness,[38] exaggerates

---

34. *See* United States v. Dispoz–O–Plastics, Inc., 172 F.3d 275, 283 (3d Cir. 1999); Gradskey v. United States, 373 F.2d 706, 710 (5th Cir. 1967).

35. *See* *Dispoz–O–Plastics,* 172 F.3d at 283; Commonwealth v. Ciampa, 406 Mass. 257, 547 N.E.2d 314, 320 (1989).

36. *See* ABA Model Rule 3.4(e); ABA Criminal Justice Standard 3–5.8(a).

37. *See* Commentary to ABA Criminal Justice Standard 3–5.8 (3rd ed. p. 107).

38. *See* United States v. Watson, 171 F.3d 695, 699 (D.C. Cir. 1999); Commonwealth v. Loguidice, 420 Mass. 453, 650 N.E.2d 1254, 1257 (1995).

factual testimony (e.g., size, quantity, distance, value),[39] alludes to uncharged and unproven prior criminal activity by the defendant[40] or suggests to the jury that the prosecutor knows pertinent facts that did not come out at trial.[41] The same rule is violated where the prosecutor urges the jury to draw an impermissible inference from evidence that the judge admitted for a limited purpose only (e.g., hearsay offered to prove "notice" argued for truth of matter asserted, or prior bad act of defendant offered for impeachment argued to prove his propensity to commit the crime).[42]

The Due Process Clause of the Fifth Amendment may be violated where the prosecutor engages in inflammatory argument calculated to raise the passions or prejudices of the jury.[43] ABA Criminal Justice Standard 3–5.8(c) similarly provides that the prosecutor "should not make arguments calculated to appeal to the prejudices of the jury." Examples of such improper argument include appealing to the jury's patriotic duty,[44] imploring the jury to protect other citizens from the public safety threat posed by the defendant,[45] asking the jury to "send a clear message" to the community by its verdict;[46] inviting the jury to vindicate the interests of the victims,[47] or injecting racial, ethic, or group biases into the jury's decision.[48] The key issue in each of these instances is whether the prosecutor improperly shifted the emphasis of his closing argument from a discussion of the factual evidence to an appeal to the jury's sympathies or emotions.[49]

---

39. *See* United States v. Donato, 99 F.3d 426 (D.C. Cir. 1996).

40. *See* Commonwealth v. Westerman, 414 Mass. 688, 611 N.E.2d 215, 224 (1993); State v. Miller, 271 N.C. 646, 157 S.E.2d 335, 344 (1967).

41. *See* United States v. Maddox, 156 F.3d 1280, 1282 (D.C. Cir. 1998); People v. Emerson, 97 Ill.2d 487, 74 Ill.Dec. 11, 455 N.E.2d 41, 45 (1983).

42. State v. VanWagner, 504 N.W.2d 746, 749 (Minn. 1993); Commonwealth v. Bassett, 21 Mass. App. Ct. 713, 490 N.E.2d 459, 461 (1986).

43. Viereck v. United States, 318 U.S. 236 (1943).

44. *Id.* at 247 (during World War II prosecutor likened juror's duty to soldiers on Bataan Peninsula).

45. *See, e.g.,* United States v. Crooks, 83 F.3d 103 (5th Cir. 1996).

46. *See* United States v. Hernandez, 865 F.2d 925, 927 (7th Cir. 1989); Commonwealth v. Mello, 420 Mass. 375, 649 N.E.2d 1106, 1111 (1995).

47. *See* Powell v. State, 995 P.2d 510 (Okla. Crim. App. 2000); Commonwealth v. Palmariello, 392 Mass. 126, 466 N.E.2d 805, 812 (1984).

48. *See, e.g.,* McFarland v. Smith, 611 F.2d 414, 416–17 (2d Cir. 1979); United States v. Sanchez, 482 F.2d 5, 9 (5th Cir. 1973).

49. United States v. Doe, 903 F.2d 16, 25 (D.C. Cir. 1990).

The Self Incrimination Clause of the Fifth Amendment has been interpreted to prohibit a prosecutor during closing argument from commenting on the defendant's failure to testify.[50] All criminal defendants are presumed to be innocent, and they have a constitutional right to put the government to its burden of proof and to decline to take the witness stand. Both *direct* and *indirect* references to a defendant's failure to testify at trial violate the Fifth Amendment; in the latter case, the court will ask whether the language used by the prosecutor was "of such a nature that the jury would naturally and necessarily view the comment as a reference to the defendant's failure to testify."[51] For example, asking rhetorically why there is "no one [who] could corroborate" an accomplice's testimony, coupled with a sweeping gesture toward the defendant seated at counsel table, has been construed to burden the defendant's constitutional protection against self incrimination.[52] Suggesting to the jury that they have heard "no other explanation" for the alleged incident, or referring to certain evidence as "uncontroverted" or "uncontested" where the defendant was in a unique position to rebut the fact, may also violate the defendant's protection against self incrimination.[53]

An important distinction must be raised between commenting on a *defendant's* failure to testify, and commenting on a defendant's failure to call *other* witnesses to support a defense. The absence of witnesses to support a defense already raised by the defendant is a fair matter for comment by the prosecutor during closing argument.[54] For example, if the defendant claims that he was holding stolen property for a relative, or that the money seized from his pocket during a drug arrest was a "loan" from a friend, the prosecutor may invite the jury to disbelieve this defense by arguing that— were the claim true—the relative or friend would have been called to the stand. The only preconditions to raising this "missing witness" argument in closing are that the witness

---

50. Griffin v. California, 380 U.S. 609, 611 (1965) (reversing murder conviction where prosecutor stated in closing that defendant "has not seen fit to take the stand and deny or explain" the killing).

51. United States v. Singer, 732 F.2d 631, 637 (8th Cir. 1984).

52. United States v. Johnston, 127 F.3d 380, 397 (5th Cir. 1997).

53. United States. v. Cotnam, 88 F.3d 487, 500 (7th Cir. 1996); Commonwealth v. Borodine, 371 Mass. 1, 353 N.E.2d 649, 655–56 (1976).

54. *See* Graves v. United States, 150 U.S. 118, 121 (1893).

must be sufficiently identified with the defendant to be considered "under his control" rather than equally available to the prosecutor, and the subject matter of the witness's testimony in light of the defense raised must reasonably be expected to aid the defendant.[55] A prosecutor may not fairly raise a "missing witness" argument where the prosecutor knows that the witness in question has asserted or would assert a Fifth Amendment privilege if called to the stand, or if criminal charges are pending or have been threatened against the witness for his involvement in the case.[56]

Finally, the defendant's Sixth Amendment right to counsel may be infringed where the prosecutor disparages the defense attorney in his closing argument. The prosecutor's proper role in closing argument is to draw the jury's attention to the testimony and exhibits, not to the tactics, demeanor, or appearance of opposing counsel. Prosecutorial misconduct has been found where the government lawyer impugned the ethics or integrity of defense counsel (such as by branding opposing counsel a "liar" or suggesting that he deliberately "mislead" the jury)[57] or where the prosecutor called into doubt the reasons that defense counsel may have interposed objections during trial (such as by suggesting that counsel intentionally tried to "distract the jury" from the true issues in the case).[58]

Where defendant claims that the prosecutor's closing argument deprived the defendant of these Fifth or Sixth Amendment protections, the conviction may be affirmed notwithstanding the prosecutorial misconduct if the court concludes that the error was harmless beyond a reasonable doubt in the context of the entire case.[59] In making a harmless error determination, the appellate tribunal will examine the likely impact of the improper argument on the jury by assessing three factors: the strength of the government's other evidence against the defendant; whether forceful curative or limiting instructions were given by the judge; and, whether the improper closing by the prosecutor was

55. NDAA Standard 85.4.

56. Gershman, PROSECUTORIAL MIS-CONDUCT at § 11:13

57. *See* Sizemore v. Fletcher, 921 F.2d 667 (6th Cir. 1990); State v. Lyles, 996 S.W.2d 713, 716 (Mo. Ct. App. 1999).

58. *See* State v. Matthews, 358 N.C. 102, 591 S.E.2d 535, 542 (2004).

59. *Young*, 470 U.S. at 11.

"invited" by improper comments of defense counsel on a related topic.[60] Under the "invited response" doctrine, a prosecutor's misstep in closing argument that was prompted by defense error may save the conviction from reversal. Some state courts have been less willing than their federal counterparts to adopt an "invited response" doctrine when evaluating a prosecutor's closing argument. Several courts have suggested that because prosecutors are ministers of justice with a heightened obligation of adversarial fairness, they must remedy defense excesses in closing argument by moving to strike the offensive comments or seeking curative instructions, rather than by attempting to fight "fire with fire."[61] Moreover, the invited response doctrine will not necessarily serve as a defense to a finding of unethical behavior by the prosecutor in administrative proceedings brought under state attorney discipline rules.[62]

E.   Demeanor in the Courtroom

A prosecutor is responsible for maintaining a respectful and dignified demeanor in the courtroom. ABA Model Rule 3.5 prohibits an attorney from engaging in conduct "intended to disrupt a tribunal." No matter how contentious the adversarial process may become, the prosecutor must remember that he is an officer of the court with a responsibility to maintain his civility during court proceedings. Vulgarity, obstreperous conduct, outbursts of temper, and personally abusive remarks directed at opposing counsel, the judge, a witness, or court staff must all be avoided. Where the prosecutor engages in such disruptive behavior, the court may punish him for contempt,[63] or may refer the incident to bar disciplinary authorities as an alleged violation of Rule 3.5.[64]

60. Darden v. Wainwright, 477 U.S. 168, 182 (1986).

61. *See* State v. Butler, 55 Conn. App. 502, 739 A.2d 732, 740 (1999); Commonwealth v. Kozec, 399 Mass. 514, 505 N.E.2d 519, 522 (1987). *See generally Berger*, 295 U.S. at 88 (suggesting that improper argument on part of prosecutor is likely to carry greater weight with jury than improper argument by defense counsel).

62. *See* State v. Pennington, 115 N.M. 372, 382, 851 P.2d 494 (1993).

63. *See* In re McGinty, 30 Ohio App.3d 219, 507 N.E.2d 441, 445–46 (1986).

64. *See* ABA Model Rule 3.5, Comment [4].

F.   Relations with the Court

The prosecutor must at all times be candid in his representations to the court regarding the subject matter of the proceedings. A lawyer may not make "false statements of fact or law" to the tribunal.[65] For example, it would violate the Rules of Professional Conduct for a prosecutor to secure a continuance by misrepresenting to the court the length of the anticipated trial, the availability of witnesses, or the presence of conflicts on the prosecutor's schedule. The prosecutor must also bring controlling legal authority to the attention of the tribunal whenever it is adverse to the position of the government and not disclosed by defense counsel.[66] If the prosecutor is aware of a statute or appellate court decision that supports the defendant's argument and is binding on the tribunal, he must cite this authority in his court filings or oral argument if defense counsel neglects to do so.

ABA Model Rule 3.5(b) prohibits a prosecutor from having any *ex parte* contact with the trial judge during the pendency of a case.[67] The prosecutor must scrupulously avoid any oral or written communications with the presiding judge on the subject of the litigation without the defense lawyer being present. At times, this rule may be difficult for prosecutors to follow due to the frequency with which they may come into contact with judges in the courthouse—in the corridors, in the cafeteria, in the elevators, and even in the courtroom while litigating other matters. Nevertheless, even the most casual conversation with the judge about an ongoing case in any of these settings is expressly prohibited. To assure fairness to the other side, a prosecutor must avoid all *ex parte* contact with the judge unless such conduct is expressly "authorized by law"[68] (such as during application for search warrants or electronic surveillance).

G.   Relations with Defense Counsel

A prosecutor should decline to accept the assignment of a case for investigation or prosecution where the defendant

---

65. ABA Model Rule 3.3(a)(1).

66. ABA Model Rule 3.3(a)(2).

67. ABA Model Rule 3.5(b). *See also* ABA Criminal Justice Standard 3–2.8(c).

68. ABA Model Rule 3.5(b).

is represented by a family member of the prosecutor (i.e., parent, child, sibling, or spouse).[69] Where the prosecutor is closely related to defense counsel by blood or marriage, there is a significant risk that the family relationship will interfere with the lawyer's independent professional judgment and duty of loyalty to the state. For similar reasons, a prosecutor should disqualify himself from prosecuting a case where he has an outside business interest with the attorney representing the defendant;[70] where he has an intimate personal relationship with defense counsel;[71] or, where he is negotiating with defense counsel's firm for future employment.[72] Although the ABA Model Rules are not as detailed as the Criminal Justice Standards on the topic of what relationships between a prosecutor and defense counsel are prohibited, the disciplinary rules define a "concurrent conflict of interest" as any "personal interest of the lawyer" that poses a "significant risk" of materially limiting the lawyer's representation of a client.[73]

A prosecutor may normally continue to represent the government in a criminal case where he has a business, family, or personal relationship with a *colleague* of the defense lawyer (e.g., a partner in the same firm, or another staff attorney in the same public defender's office) or where another assistant district attorney in the same prosecutor's office has the proscribed relationship with defense counsel.[74] Disqualifications arising from personal relationships "ordinarily [are] not imputed to members of firms with whom the

---

69. ABA Criminal Justice Standard 3–1.3(g); NDAA Standard 7.3(c).

70. NDAA Standard 7.3(c).

71. *See* People v. Jackson, 167 Cal. App.3d 829, 832, 213 Cal.Rptr. 521 (1985) (reversing conviction for ineffective assistance of defense counsel where prosecutor and defense attorney were involved in sustained dating relationship). *Cf.* ABA Criminal Justice Standard 3–1.3(g) (allowing prosecutor to continue to represent the state where he has a "significant personal or financial relationship" with the defense lawyer, provided the prosecutor's supervisor consents after full disclosure).

72. ABA Model Rule 1.11(d)(2)(ii); ABA Criminal Justice Standard 3–1.3(e).

73. *See* ABA Model Rule 1.7(a).

74. *See* Comm. On Prof'l Ethics of the Conn. Bar Ass'n., Op. 86–15 (1986) (prosecutor and public defender who were married could handle cases in same court division so long as they did not directly oppose each other); Prof'l Ethics Commission of the Board of Overseers of the Me. Bar, Op. 42 (1983) (prosecutor not barred from representing state where defendant was represented by his spouse's law partner).

lawyers are associated."[75] Courts have thus been reluctant to disqualify an entire prosecutor's office based on the personal relationship of one assistant district attorney with the defendant or his counsel.[76] However, where another lawyer in the prosecutor's office has a business, family, or personal relationship with the defendant or his counsel, the prosecutor assigned to the case must avoid sharing any information or material regarding the ongoing case with his "screened" colleague.[77]

A highly complex and problematic issue for prosecutors during the course of a criminal trial is whether and how to respond to defense counsel who appears to be advocating ineffectively for his client. This issue may arise when defense counsel fails to file a meritorious motion to suppress or dismiss, neglects an important line of questioning on cross examination of a key government witness, or appears in court to be under the influence of alcohol or narcotic substances. In each of these situations, the prosecutor must step out of his role as a pure advocate to insure that the defendant receives a fair trial. To ignore ineffective lawyering by defense counsel risks not only convicting an innocent person, but also wasting public resources litigating post-conviction claims that trial counsel's performance fell below the standard of "effective assistance of counsel" guaranteed by the Sixth and Fourteenth Amendments.[78]

The ethical rules and standards are conspicuously silent on a prosecutor's professional responsibilities in the face of substandard advocacy by an opponent, beyond the broad admonition in Comment [1] to Model Rule 3.8 that a prosecutor must act as a "minister of justice." One option is for the prosecutor to take defense counsel aside, point out the defects in his advocacy, and ask him to consider seeking leave to withdraw from the case if he is unable or unwilling

---

75. ABA Model Rule 1.7, Comment [11].

76. *See* State v. Jones, 180 Conn. 443, 429 A.2d 936, 942 (1980); State v. Fitzpatrick, 464 So.2d 1185, 1188 (Fla. 1985). *Cf.* Commonwealth v. Croken, 432 Mass. 266, 733 N.E.2d 1005, 1012 (2000) (ordering evidentiary hearing to determine whether defendant's constitutional right to effective assistance of counsel was violated by defense attorney's personal relationship with an assistant prosecutor in the same office that handled the matter against the accused).

77. State v. Pennington, 115 N.M. 372, 851 P.2d 494, 501 (1993).

78. Strickland v. Washington, 466 U.S. 668, 686 (1984).

to improve his performance. Another option is for the prosecutor to compensate for defense counsel's inadequacies by introducing evidence favorable to the defendant on redirect examination of government witnesses, and then arguing against the significance of this information where appropriate in closing argument. A third option—advocated by several prominent scholars—is for the prosecutor to report the defense lawyer's inadequate representation to the presiding judge, possibly by filing a motion to disqualify counsel, or by asking the court to inquire of counsel on the record whether his failure to pursue certain lines of defense was a knowing and strategic decision.[79]

All three of these approaches is fraught with awkwardness and practical difficulties; they each presume 1) that there are no reasonable tactical explanation for defense counsel's behavior, and 2) that the prosecutor is in a better position to ascertain the interests of the defendant than his own counsel. More fundamentally, a prosecutor need not undertake to remedy poor performance by defense counsel in any of these manners unless he is convinced that the legal representation might rise to the level of *constitutional* inadequacy. Merely because the defense attorney is less qualified or vigorous than the prosecutor does not give rise to "ineffective assistance" within the meaning of the constitutional guarantee, because the Sixth Amendment tolerates a "wide range of professionally competent assistance."[80]

The duty to remedy ineffective advocacy at trial is related to, but distinct from, a prosecutor's obligation to report ethical violations by a criminal defense lawyer to the appropriate bar disciplinary committee. Some 40 states adhere to what is colloquially referred to as the "Snitch Rule" recommended by ABA Model Rule 8.3(a); that is, a lawyer who, through unprivileged communications, *"knows* that another lawyer has committed a violation of the Rules of Professional Conduct" has an ethical duty to report that violation to the appropriate professional body if the violation "raises a *substantial* question as to that lawyer's honesty,

79. Monroe Freedman, LAWYERS' ETHICS IN AN ADVERSARY SYSTEM, 88–89 (1975); Fred C. Zacharias, *Structuring the Ethics of Prosecutorial Trial Prac-* *tice: Can Prosecutors Do Justice?,* 44 VAND. L. REV. 45, 74 (1991).

80. *Strickland,* 466 U.S. at 690.

trustworthiness, or fitness as a lawyer in other respects." A prosecutor's obligation under Rule 8.3(a) differs from his obligation to insure a fair adversarial process in two critical respects. First, where a prosecutor has knowledge that defense counsel has violated a disciplinary rule, the prosecutor has an obligation to report that violation to the bar disciplinary authority, not to the court presiding over the criminal proceeding. Second, the professional obligation to act as a whistleblower for misconduct committed by other lawyers applies only where the violation is so egregious that it raises a *"substantial* question" about the lawyer's fitness to practice law *"in other respects."* Isolated acts of incompetence by defense counsel in an individual case may trigger the prosecutor's duty to take appropriate steps to insure a fair trial,[81] without giving rise to an obligation to report the matter to bar disciplinary authorities.

PROBLEMS

1. Assistant District Attorney Jennifer Ferreira is prosecuting a charge of assault and battery on a police officer. The defendant, a young African American male, is charged with punching a white police officer during a routine "stop and frisk." The arrest occurred in a high crime area of the city targeted by the police for drug dealing. A member of the venire is an African American woman who lives with her three teenage children in the same section of the city. The neighborhood is predominantly minority. The prosecutor is concerned that this prospective juror may be sympathetic to the plight of the defendant, or that her teenage children may have had similar negative encounters with the police. She challenges the prospective juror. When the prosecutor is asked by the judge for a reason, the prosecutor states that because the juror lives in the same section of the city as the defendant, "she may identify with his situation." Is that a race neutral, case-based reason that will survive a *Batson* challenge?

2. Assistant U.S. Attorney Jack Kelly is prosecuting an arson case. Agents from the Bureau of Alcohol, Tobacco, and Firearms investigated the fire scene using an accelerant-detecting canine. The dog "alerted" on the presence of gasoline, and subsequent laboratory testing proved that an accelerant was used at the

---

81. *See* ABA Model Rule 1.1 ("A lawyer shall provide competent representation to a client.")

site. The prosecutor wants to have the ATF agent testify to how his canine was used in the investigation, and actually to have the dog demonstrate its detection techniques in the courtroom during the agent's testimony. The prosecutor knows of no other occasion when such an "animal demonstration" has been allowed in federal courts in his district, although it has been allowed in other jurisdictions. May the AUSA refer to the canine's expected "testimony" during his opening statement?

3. Assistant District Attorney Abbe Ross is prosecuting a drug case. The defendant was arrested when police, armed with a search warrant, entered his apartment and seized one kilogram of cocaine and extensive drug paraphernalia. At a motion to suppress, the police officer who applied for the search warrant testified that immediately prior to the warrant's execution, he entered the apartment in an undercover capacity to purchase a small quantity of cocaine (in order to "freshen up" the information in the warrant). The police officer testifies that he was alone. The motion to suppress is denied.

Four months later, the case is ready for trial. The prosecutor is preparing the police officer to testify by reviewing his prior testimony at the grand jury and the motion to suppress. During trial preparation, the officer tells the prosecutor that during the "freshen up" buy he was actually accompanied by a confidential informant. He did not disclose this fact during his testimony during the motion to suppress hearing, because he was afraid that the judge would order him to disclose the informant's identity.

The prosecutor now realizes that his witness perjured himself on a prior occasion in the same case. The officer begs the prosecutor to keep this information "just between us." Should the prosecutor disclose the prior perjury to the defense counsel? To the court? Does the answer depend on whether the prosecutor intends to call the same police officer to testify at trial? What if the prosecutor can prove the case by calling other police officers instead?

4. Assistant District Attorney Jeremy Silverfine is prosecuting a narcotics case. The defendant takes the stand and puts forth an entrapment defense. The defendant testifies that he is of Cuban descent, and that his family came to the United States to flee the Castro regime. On cross examination, the prosecutor attempts to impeach the defendant's credibility. The prosecutor has a vague memory that the landlord of the defendant's apartment building told him during a telephone interview that the defendant indicated on his lease that he was from Colombia. May the prosecutor confront the defendant about this lie on cross

examination? Does it depend on whether the landlord is available to testify? Whether the lease is available for introduction in evidence?

5.   In a murder prosecution, the defense counsel in closing argument states that the police officers who testified at trial should not be believed, because "the police lie—you know they lie—you read the papers. Two of their fellow officers were indicted just last week for extorting money from arrested persons." The prosecutor objects and moves to strike this argument. The judge allows the motion to strike and instructs the jury not to consider any comments by defense counsel on facts not in evidence. In the prosecutor's closing argument, she states "There is no evidence before you that these two police officers involved in this case had any motive to lie. They are two of the finest police officers that I have ever worked with." Is this improper?

CHAPTER EIGHT

THE PROSECUTOR AND THE PRESS

The ethical rules pertaining to lawyer speech attempt to strike a balance between protecting the rights of the accused to a fair trial, and safeguarding all citizen's rights to expression and the free flow of information. A prosecutor's comments to the media can serve worthwhile and legitimate purposes relating to the conduct of government. However, a prosecutor's extra-judicial comments can also jeopardize a defendant's right to a fair trial by implanting suggestions of guilt in the minds of the public before the charges can be fully and fairly exposed in a court of law. Protecting a prosecutor's right to speak while simultaneously ensuring that the defendant is not tried, convicted and sentenced in the court of public opinion requires a difficult but critical balancing of competing interests.[1]

Notwithstanding the First Amendment's guarantee of freedom of speech, there are serious countervailing concerns relating to the administration of criminal justice which warrant some curtailment of a prosecutor's public comments.[2] First, public dissemination of information about the crime in advance of trial risks undercutting the presumption of innocence to which all defendants are entitled. Society (and potential jurors) may be convinced of the defendant's guilt before the matter ever proceeds to trial. Second, statements to the media risk irreparably destroying the defendant's reputation and ability to earn a livelihood. Even if the accused is subsequently acquitted of the charges against

---

1. *See* In re Conduct of Lasswell, 296 Or. 121, 673 P.2d 855, 857 (1983).

2. *See* Scott M. Matheson, *The Prosecutor, the Press, and Free Speech*, 58 FORDHAM L. REV. 865, 868 (1990).

him, he may be forever tainted by the accusation of wrong-doing leveled against him by the government. Finally, media coverage of the prosecutor's allegations may interfere with a defendant's fifth amendment right to remain silent. If the government's theory of its case is widely broadcast, the defendant may feel compelled to respond rather than to remain silent and put the government to its burden of proof. For all of these reasons, some curtailment of lawyer speech is seen as necessary to safeguard the fairness and accuracy of the adjudicative process.

There are several important and legitimate reasons why a prosecutor may feel compelled to talk to the media about the activities of his office. First, the public has a right to be kept informed about how a prosecutor is using public re-sources, and what choices he is making about enforcement priorities. "[T]he subject matter of legal proceedings is often of direct significance in debate and deliberation over ques-tions of public policy."[3] As a public servant, the prosecutor has a fiduciary obligation to apprise his constituents of how he is managing the trust that they have placed in him. Second, a prosecutor's public comments to the media may promote public safety by warning the public of continuing dangers in the community, or cautioning them about partic-ularly vulnerable activities or sources of risk. Third, public statements by prosecutors may assist in ongoing investiga-tions by encouraging witnesses or other victims to come forward to report crime. Prosecutors often utilize the press to request public assistance in catching criminals who might otherwise remain at large. Finally, public dissemination of a prosecutor's activities is necessary to allow the criminal law to fulfill its deterrent aims; unless the public is notified about indictments and convictions, other would-be perpetra-tors will not be dissuaded from engaging in similar behavior. Prosecutors have an interest in developing good relation-ships with the press because the media serves as a vital conduit of information both to and from the public.

Notwithstanding these proper motives, there are equally pervasive but less legitimate reasons why a prosecutor may choose to talk to the media about pending criminal cases. The prosecutor may issue public statements in order to gain

3. ABA Model Rule 3.6, Comment [1].

a tactical advantage at trial by tainting the prospective jury pool with highly inflammatory and one-sided presentation of the alleged facts. The prosecutor might utilize the media to try to leverage a guilty plea from the defendant by exposing him to public ridicule and embarrassment. The prosecutor may be utilizing a high-profile prosecution for political advantage—such as to increase his chances of re-election, or to seek revenge against a political enemy. Even a low-level staff prosecutor may see potential for career advancement in a high profile case assigned to him, and may attempt to parlay his involvement in the case into a judgeship, appointment to other government office, or a movie or book contract.

Recognizing both the legitimate and the illegitimate interests served by attorney speech, the Model Rules of Professional Conduct take an approach to this issue that accommodates public comments by lawyers so long as they do not pose a serious risk to the judicial process. ABA Model Rule 3.6 provides that a lawyer participating in the investigation or litigation of a matter shall not make statements that "the lawyer knows or reasonably should know will be disseminated by means of public communication and will have a substantial likelihood of materially prejudicing a proceeding in the matter."

Rule 3.6 has three components. First, the attorney must know or have reason to know that his statement about the case will be "disseminated" publicly. Making a statement about a pending case to a acquaintance during a private dinner party is not covered by the rule, even if the acquaintance later repeats the statement to a reporter without the prosecutor's authorization. But making the same statement on the steps of the courthouse *is* covered by the rule, if a crowd is present, or if the lawyer "reasonably should know" that a member of the media may be in attendance covering the event. Second, the rule constrains the public speech only of attorneys involved in the adjudicative matter "or their associates;"[4] outside lawyers are not prohibited from making public comments about pending cases (such as by serving as a media advisor or "commentator" during a pending trial) so long as they have no direct involvement in representing a party or witness in the litigation. Finally, Rule 3.6 looks not

---

4. ABA Model Rule 3.6, Comment [3].

to potential disparagement of the *defendant*, but rather to the likely impact of the public statement on the outcome of the *proceeding*. Only those statements that the lawyer has reason to know will have "substantial likelihood" of materially prejudicing the proceeding are prohibited by the rule. Because judges have ample discretion to "cure" any adverse effects of pre-trial publicity before the commencement of an adjudicative process (such as by moving the location of the trial, using voir dire to screen out potential jurors who have read or heard about the case, or asking the jurors whether they have abided by their oath not to listen to media accounts of the trial) this high standard of "substantial likelihood" leaves both prosecutors and defense lawyers ample room to make pre-trial public statements without violating their ethical responsibilities.[5]

In *Gentile v. State Bar of Nevada*,[6] a case involving speech by a criminal defense attorney, the Supreme Court ruled that the "substantial likelihood of material prejudice" standard evoked in Model Rule 3.6 satisfies the First Amendment. Even though ethical rules restricting attorney speech are content based rather than content neutral, the Court ruled that attorneys are "officers of the court" with an obligation to safeguard the integrity of judicial proceedings. Restrictions on attorney speech about pending cases may therefore be regulated under a less exacting standard than the "clear and present danger" test that content-based regulations of the press must normally satisfy.[7] Nonetheless, five justices in *Gentile* joined in a section of Justice Kennedy's opinion ruling that the Nevada version of Rule 3.6 then in effect was void for vagueness, because its use of the terms "general nature of the . . . defense" in defining a safe harbor provision for attorney speech left too much room for interpretation and prejudicial application.[8]

---

5. *See* Stroble v. California, 343 U.S. 181, 191–92 (1952) (prosecutor's statements to media about post-arrest confession of alleged child killer did not render subsequent trial unfair, because six week gap between statements and trial gave the court ample opportunity to cure any potential prejudice through jury selection and instruction).

6. 501 U.S. 1030 (1991).

7. *Id*. at 1073. Although some sections of Chief Justice Rehnquist's opinion commanded the votes of only four justices, Justice O'Connor joined in the section concerning the standard to be applied to lawyer speech under the First Amendment, making that section a majority opinion. *Id*. at 1081.

8. *Id*. at 1048.

Most state discipline codes contain restrictions on attorney speech similar to the "substantial likelihood of material prejudice" standard contained in ABA Model Rule 3.6(a).[9] In fact, the justices in *Gentile* strongly suggested that any meaningfully broader definition of prejudice—such as the "*reasonably* likely to interfere with a fair trial" standard previously utilized in ABA Model Code of Professional Responsibility provision 7–107(D)—might not serve a compelling state interest sufficient to survive First Amendment scrutiny.[10] Illinois and the District of Columbia prohibit public statements that would pose a "serious and *imminent*" threat to pending court proceedings, which suggest perhaps an even narrower restriction on attorney speech than the ABA Model Rule.[11]

The commentary to ABA Model Rule 3.6 contains a list of six topics that ordinarily will be considered "more likely than not to have a material prejudicial effect on a proceeding." Lawyers associated with the prosecution or defense of a criminal matter should scrupulously avoid making public statements concerning the following "off limit" topics: (1) the character, reputation, credibility, or prior criminal record of a witness or party; (2) the possibility of a plea of guilty; (3) the contents of any confession; (4) the performance or results of any examination or test (or the failure of a person to submit to an examination or test); (5) the lawyer's personal opinion about the guilt or innocence of the defendant; and (6) any evidence or information that the lawyer knows is likely to be inadmissible at trial.[12] The National District Attorneys' Association suggests that prosecutors should not publicly release any facts relating to these same six categories of information.[13] In addition, Comment [5] to Rule 3.6 contains an admonition that a lawyer should not make a public statement announcing that a defendant has been charged with a crime unless that statement is accompanied by an explanation "that the charge is merely an accusa-

9. Matheson, *supra* ch. 8 n.2, at 873.

10. *See* 501 U.S. at 1036–37 (opinion of Kennedy, J.).

11. D.C. Rule of Prof'l Conduct 3.6; Ill. Rule of Prof'l Conduct 3.6(a).

12. ABA Model Rule 3.6, comment [5]. *See* Attorney Grievance Commission v. Gansler, 377 Md. 656, 835 A.2d 548, 569 (2003) (reprimanding State's Attorney for making public comments about suspect's post arrest confession and possibility of plea bargain).

13. NDAA Standard 34.2.

tion and that the defendant is presumed innocent until and unless proven guilty."[14]

Many of the "off limit" topics set forth in the comment to Rule 3.6 are directed at public reference to evidence that may turn out to be inadmissible at trial (witness impeachment material, forensic tests, confessions). The concern is that once such influential material finds its way into the public domain, the defendant may not be able to receive a fair trial from an impartial jury, even if the evidence is later excluded. However, one of the "off limit" topics presumptively prohibited by ABA Model Rule 3.6, Comment [5] is highly controversial, and may not survive a First Amendment attack were it to be challenged by a prosecutor disciplined under the provisions of that section. Comment [5](3) suggests that it is "more likely than not" prejudicial for a lawyer to make public comment about the "performance or results of any examination" or *the identity or nature of physical evidence expected to be presented.*" This section goes well beyond its predecessor, Model Code provision 7–107(C), which specifically allowed public comment describing "physical evidence seized" by law enforcement "at the time of seizure," so long as the evidence did not relate to a "confession, admission, or statement." It certainly is not uncommon for prosecutors and/or the police to display seized evidence at a press conference announcing an arrest or indictment, such as a large cache of narcotics, seized weapons, or other contraband. The NDAA standards do not bar public comment on physical evidence at the time of arrest or seizure.[15] Surely physical evidence, like a confession or a forensic test, might be suppressed by the court and never admitted at trial. But in many circumstances, such physical evidence is unlikely to have as prejudicial impact on the accused, because unlike a confession or a fingerprint it may not be inextricably linked to the defendant. Moreover, seized evidence is often directly related to matters concerning public safety, about which the community has a right to be kept informed.[16] States that follow the Model Code of Professional

---

14. ABA Model Rule 3.6, comment [5].

15. *See* NDAA Standard 34.2.

16. "The public has a right to know about threats to its safety and measures aimed at assuring its security." ABA Model Rule 3.6, Comment [1].

Responsibility approach allow public comments by the prosecutor describing seized physical evidence.[17]

Experience suggests that many types of "presumptively prejudicial" material referenced in the comments to Rule 3.6 are frequently reported in the media—including the prior criminal record of an accused, the fact or content of a confession made upon arrest, or ballistic or other forensic test results. Does this imply that prosecutors are routinely flouting their ethical obligations? One answer to this question is that the media have an important source of information about criminal investigations that is unconstrained by the Rules of Professional Conduct: that is, the police. The ethical rules relating to the practice of law govern only attorneys. Police can—and often do—make statements to the media upon the arrest of a suspect that would be prohibited if made by the prosecutor's office. While lawyers may in some situations be responsible for the conduct of non-lawyer assistants "employed or retained" by the lawyer,[18] a lawyer cannot be disciplined for the activities of independent parties unless the lawyer directly solicited or encouraged that party to engage in conduct that would be unethical if performed by the lawyer.[19]

Although prosecutors do not normally control the activities of independent police agencies, they certainly work hand in hand with police investigators and are in a good position to have some influence over the conduct of police affairs. The second paragraph of ABA Model Rule 3.8(f), derived from ABA Criminal Justice Standard 3–1.4, recognizes this reality, and mandates that prosecutors "exercise reasonable care" to prevent "law enforcement personnel" working on a case from making extrajudicial statements that the prosecutor would be prohibited from making under the disciplinary rules. This provision attempts to insure that prosecutors exert some positive influence over media comments by the police, rather than turning a blind eye toward the dissemination of material that may prove prejudicial to an ongoing criminal proceeding.

---

17. *See, e.g.,* Iowa Code Ann. R. 32, DR–7–107; Neb. R. Prof'l Responsibility 7–107(c); N.Y.R. Prof'l Responsibility DR 7–107(c).

18. *See* ABA Model Rule 5.3(c).

19. *See* ABA Model Rule 8.4(a) (it is professional misconduct for a lawyer to violate the rules "through the acts of another").

The text of Model Rule 3.6 also contains a list of subjects that lawyers are *permitted* to discuss with the media. Unlike the prohibited topics referenced in the commentary to the rule, which are considered *presumptively* prejudicial, the list of topics permissible for public comment guarantees a lawyer a "safe harbor" against attorney discipline. Model Rule 3.6(b) provides that "notwithstanding" the prohibitions of paragraph (a), a lawyer "may state:" the nature of the claim or defense involved; any information contained in a public record; that an investigation of a matter is in progress; the scheduling of any step in the court proceeding; a request for assistance in obtaining evidence; a warning to the public of any danger; and, in a criminal case, the identity, residence, occupation and family status of the accused, the time and place of arrest, the identity of investigating agents, and information necessary to aid in the apprehension of any suspects. These permissible topics of public comment are all linked to the legitimate need to inform the public about the general conduct of criminal proceedings and governmental affairs.

The broadest of these so called "safe harbor" provisions is the "public record" exception. Once information is filed in court, such as by an indictment, pleading, motion, or memorandum of law, it becomes a matter of "public record" open to discussion. Some commentators have suggested that this creates an overly large loophole for prosecutors to get prejudicial information before the public (such as the prior criminal behavior of the accused, or the results of scientific tests). For example, a prosecutor may allude to prior convictions or uncharged criminal activity in an indictment or other court papers, and once that document is filed in court it arguably becomes a matter of "public record" open to comment by the government lawyer.[20]

A second "safe-harbor" for media statements is contained in Model Rule 3.6(c), which allows a lawyer to make a statement that a reasonable lawyer "would believe is required to protect a client from the substantial undue prejudicial effect of recent publicity" not initiated by the lawyer or

---

20. Green, *Prosecutorial Ethics as Usual, supra* ch. 7 n.27, 1595–96. *See Gansler*, 835 A.2d at 569 (adopting narrow definition of public record for purposes of Maryland Rule of Professional Conduct 3.6).

his client. A criminal defense lawyer may be shielded from possible sanction under Rule 3.6 if his comments to the media are responsive to adverse publicity about the defendant generated by others, including the prosecutor, the police, and civilian witnesses. "When prejudicial statements have been publicly made by others, responsive statements may have the salutary effect of lessening any resulting adverse impact on the adjudicative proceeding."[21] This safe harbor essentially allows defense attorneys to "fight fire with fire" in the media if damaging claims have been made against their client by others. For example, it may be appropriate for a defense attorney, following intense adverse publicity resulting from the indictment of his client on a high profile matter, to reveal to the media that his client took and passed a polygraph examination, or that a key eyewitness to the crime has a history of mental illness, both matters which otherwise would be considered "presumptively" prejudicial under Comment [5] to Rule 3.6.[22] However, prosecutors would be imprudent to rely on the "fair reply" protections of Rule 3.6(c). Since prosecutors represent society at large and not individual "clients," public comments to the media responsive to criticisms leveled at the government are unlikely to ever be considered necessary to "protect a client" within a natural reading of Rule 3.6(c).[23]

While Rule 3.6 is directed at public statements by lawyers that may prejudice the outcome of an adjudicative *proceeding*, a separate provision of the Model Rules applicable only to prosecutors prohibits public communications that would unnecessarily disparage the *accused*. ABA Model Rule

---

21. ABA Model Rule 3.6, Comment [7].

22. Nevada's version of Rule 3.6 in effect in 1990 did not contain a "fair reply" provision similar to Model Rule 3.8(c). Justice Kennedy's opinion for the court in *Gentile* noted that defense counsel's comments to the media following the indictment of his client were protected speech because they "sought only to stop a wave of publicity he perceived as prejudicing potential jurors against his client and injuring his client's reputation in the communi-

ty." Subdivision (c) was added to Model Rule 3.6 in 1994 following this admonition in *Gentile*.

23. H. Richard Uviller, *Evidence from the Mind of the Criminal Suspect: A Reconsideration of the Current Rules of Access and Restraint*, 87 COLUM. L. REV. 1137, 1179–80 (1987) (arguing that prosecutor "has no client" except society at large, and that his paramount obligation is "to promote a just outcome, not a partisan victory").

3.8(f) ("Special Responsibilities of a Prosecutor") provides
that

> "[E]xcept for statements that are necessary to inform
> the public of the nature and extent of the prosecutor's
> action and that serve a legitimate law enforcement
> purpose," a prosecutor in a criminal case shall "refrain
> from making extrajudicial comments that have a sub-
> stantial likelihood of heightening public condemnation
> of the accused...."

According to the 1994 ABA Report recommending this
amendment to Model Rule 3.8, the revision was designed to
prohibit "gratuitous comments" by a prosecutor serving
only to increase "public opprobrium" toward the defendant.[24] Examples of such "piling on" that may be construed
to serve no legitimate public purpose might include a description of graphic details about a particularly gruesome or
heinous crime, the display of shocking or disturbing physical
evidence, or reference to prior bad acts or criminal associations of the accused. The comment to Rule 3.8(f) states that
"nothing in this Comment is intended to restrict the statements which a prosecutor may make which comply with [the
safe harbor provisions] of Rule 3.6(b) or 3.6(c)." Thus, a
prosecutor who makes a statement to the press about information contained in a public record (such as an indictment,
brief, or legal memoranda) cannot be disciplined under Rule
3.8(f) if his conduct otherwise complies with the safe harbor
provision of Rule 3.6(b).

A prosecutor must also abide by any additional restrictions on media contact imposed by the court during the
pendency of criminal proceedings. From the return of the
indictment until the completion of trial and sentencing, the
judge presiding over a trial has the authority to impose
restrictions on medial comments that go beyond the general
restrictions contained in the Rules of Professional Conduct.
In *Sheppard v. Maxwell*[25] the Supreme Court recognized the
inherent authority of a court to protect the defendant's right
to a fair trial by entering so-called "gag orders" prohibiting
public comments by the lawyers, parties, or witnesses involved in a case. If a gag order is entered by the court, it
may preclude comment by the attorneys to the media on

---

24. Gillers and Simon, Regulation
of Lawyers, Statutes and Standards at
250 (Aspen 2004).

25. 384 U.S. 333 (1966).

such specifics as the merits of case, the characterization of facts or legal theories, or the content of witness testimony.[26] Where a prosecutor violates a gag order issued prior to or during the trial, he can be punished for criminal contempt with sanctions ranging from reprimand to fine or imprisonment.

The prosecutor must also avoid making any statements to the media which are unfairly critical of the presiding judge. Attorneys are free to criticize the actions of jurists; in fact, discourse critical of governmental affairs is central to First Amendment protections. Nonetheless, criticism by an attorney of the judge's rulings may become censurable where it "becomes personally abusive or lacks any factual basis."[27] ABA Model Rule 8.2 provides that a lawyer "shall not make a statement that the lawyer knows to be false or with reckless disregard as to its truth or falsity concerning the qualifications or integrity of a judge." Moreover, ABA Model Rule 8.4(d) prohibits conduct "prejudicial to the administration of justice." Even comments about judges that have a seed of truth may be considered to violate the latter standard, if they are made in a highly offensive, abusive, or excoriating manner.[28]

After a verdict, the prosecutor should avoid any statements that may be interpreted as critical of the tribunal's decision in the case. This is particularly important when the jury returns an acquittal after a high-profile and hard fought case. As a advocate, the prosecutor's natural tendency may be to continue to argue the strength of his case to the media, and urge before the press the correctness of the position which the government asserted and lost. But the prosecutor must be always mindful of the fact that his primary obligation is to seek the truth, and the truth in our system of

26. *See, e.g.,* United States v. Brown, 218 F.3d 415 (5th Cir. 2000); United States v. Koubriti, 305 F.Supp.2d 723 (E.D. Mich. 2003).

27. Committee on Legal Ethics v. Douglas, 179 W.Va. 490, 370 S.E.2d 325, 328 (1988). *See* In re Sawyer, 360 U.S. 622, 646 (1959) (state could constitutionally regulate speech impugning integrity of judge, but court found speech at issue did not rise to that level).

28. *See* In the Matter of Guy, 756 A.2d 875 (Del. 2000) (accusing judge of racism); Committee on Legal Ethics v. Douglas, 179 W.Va. 490, 370 S.E.2d 325 (1988) (statement to press indicating "disdain and contempt" for ruling of court and accusing judge of "power jockeying"). *See also* ABA Criminal Justice Standard 3–5.2 (requiring lawyer to support the "dignity" of the trial court).

justice is whatever an unbiased finder of fact decides after a fair trial. As an official with responsibilities in the criminal justice system, the prosecutor should not exhibit disrespect for the institution that rendered the decision. Public faith in the criminal justice system requires government officials to be willing to support the outcome of a fairly conducted trial, whether the jury determines that the defendant is guilty or not guilty. While a prosecutor may acknowledge his "disappointment" in the verdict, he should not suggest that the jury was wrong in their decision, or that they failed to fulfill their duties conscientiously. Toward that end, ABA Criminal Justice Standard 3–5.10 provides that a "prosecutor should not make public comments critical of a verdict, whether rendered by judge or jury."

Finally, a prosecutor must avoid entering into any literary contracts with respect to a case until after the criminal matter is completed through appeal. Model Rule 1.8(d) provides that "[p]rior to the conclusion of his representation of a client, a lawyer shall not make or negotiate an agreement giving the lawyer literary or media rights of a portrayal or account based in substantial part on information relating to the representation." The purpose of this rule is to avoid the divided loyalties that may result when a lawyer is actively pursuing a book or movie deal about a case during the conduct of litigation. In those situations, a conflict of interest could arise between the lawyer's financial interests and the interest of his client, because "[m]easures suitable in the representation of a client may detract from the publication value of an account of the representation." Although an argument could be made that this rule has no application to prosecutors due to the rule's use of the term "client," the dangers of divided loyalty posed by media contracts are acutely present for government lawyers in criminal cases. For example, a prosecutor might decline to propose a reasonable and legitimate plea bargain in a criminal case that may be in the best interests of justice, if he wanted to insure a trial in order to provide fodder for a book or film under contract. ABA Standard for Criminal Justice 3–2.11 suggests a restriction on literary or media agreements by prosecutors during the pendency of the proceedings essentially identical to Model Rule 1.8.

PROBLEMS

1. Assistant District Attorney Michael Zullas has just indicted a prominent local politician on charges of statutory rape relating to allegations that he molested his family's fourteen-year-old babysitter. During the course of the investigation, the defendant declined, through counsel, to be interviewed or to appear before the grand jury. Defense counsel did propose a polygraph examination, which the prosecutor scheduled for the defendant at the State Police Crime Lab; however, the defendant and his counsel failed to show up on the date scheduled for the exam.

     a. At arraignment, the prosecutor argues for appropriate conditions of bail, citing as one factor relating to dangerousness the defendant's conviction twenty years earlier on a charge of lewd and lascivious behavior. Upon returning to his office following the arraignment, the prosecutor gets a call from a reporter for the major local newspaper. The reporter says "I missed the arraignment. Can you tell me if this guy has a record?" Is the prosecutor free to repeat to the reporter what he said in open court about the defendant's prior conviction?

     b. The reporter also tells the prosecutor over the telephone that he has just finished a conversation with defense counsel, who called the prosecution "politically motivated" and "an outrage." According to the reporter, defense counsel said that "defendant was never alone with the youth on the dates in question, and that the victim was a compulsive liar and drug abuser." Defense counsel also told the reporter that "the police never even interviewed my guy to find out his side of the story. My client offered to be polygraphed, but the government was so busy pursuing its political vendetta against my client that it didn't bother with the truth!" Is the prosecutor free to correct the misstatement allegedly made by defense counsel, by pointing out that the defendant asserted his Fifth Amendment rights and declined both to testify before the grand jury and to submit to a polygraph examination?

2. A terrorist has bombed a courthouse in the state capitol. Assistant District Attorney Paula DeGiacomo is the prosecutor assigned to the investigation. The day following the explosion, the police receive an anonymous letter from a radical, quasi-religious terrorist organization claiming responsibility for the bombing, stating that it was in retaliation for a recent pro-choice ruling by the state's highest court. The letter is anonymous.

a.   Before the prosecutor has had a chance to corroborate the letter's claim of responsibility or to ascertain its authenticity, may she alert the public to the possibility that a terrorist group may have been involved?

b.   Assume that the prosecutor's investigation confirms the existence of the terrorist group and ascertains its membership and leadership. Based upon the letter and law enforcement's investigation to date, the prosecutor assists the police in applying for, and obtaining, a warrant to search the home of the group's leader. The affidavit in support of the search warrant, which has been lodged at the local district court in the town where the leader resides, details the group's composition and its activities. When the police raid the house, the media get wind of the search, and suspect that it may have something to do with the courthouse bombing. A reporter calls the prosecutor and asks her for details of the search and the information contained in the affidavit. May the prosecutor disclose to the reporter the facts contained in the search warrant application? May she disclose to the reporter what was seized at the group leader's home during the execution of the search warrant?

APPENDIX A

AMERICAN BAR ASSOCIATION MODEL RULES OF PROFESSIONAL RESPONSIBILITY

SELECT PROVISIONS[1]

RULE 3.3   CANDOR TO THE TRIBUNAL

(a) A lawyer shall not knowingly:

(1) make a false statement of fact or law to a tribunal or fail to correct a false statement of material fact or law previously made to the tribunal by the lawyer;

(2) fail to disclose to the tribunal legal authority in the controlling jurisdiction known to the lawyer to be directly adverse to the position of the client and not disclosed by opposing counsel; or

(3) offer evidence that the lawyer knows to be false. If a lawyer, the lawyer's client, or a witness called by the lawyer, has offered material evidence and the lawyer comes to know of its falsity, the lawyer shall take reasonable remedial measures, including, if necessary, disclosure to the tribunal. A lawyer may refuse to offer evidence, other than the testimony of a defendant in a criminal matter, that the lawyer reasonably believes is false.

(b) A lawyer who represents a client in an adjudicative proceeding and who knows that a person intends to engage, is engaging or has engaged in criminal or

1. Reprinted with the permission of the American Bar Association, 321 North Clark Street, Chicago, Illinois.

fraudulent conduct related to the proceeding shall take reasonable remedial measures, including, if necessary, disclosure to the tribunal.

(c) The duties stated in paragraphs (a) and (b) continue to the conclusion of the proceeding, and apply even if compliance requires disclosure of information otherwise protected by Rule 1.6.

(d) In an ex parte proceeding, a lawyer shall inform the tribunal of all material facts known to the lawyer that will enable the tribunal to make an informed decision, whether or not the facts are adverse.

Comment

[1]   This Rule governs the conduct of a lawyer who is representing a client in the proceedings of a tribunal. See Rule 1.0(m) for the definition of "tribunal." It also applies when the lawyer is representing a client in an ancillary proceeding conducted pursuant to the tribunal's adjudicative authority, such as a deposition. Thus, for example, paragraph (a)(3) requires a lawyer to take reasonable remedial measures if the lawyer comes to know that a client who is testifying in a deposition has offered evidence that is false.

[2]   This Rule sets forth the special duties of lawyers as officers of the court to avoid conduct that undermines the integrity of the adjudicative process. A lawyer acting as an advocate in an adjudicative proceeding has an obligation to present the client's case with persuasive force. Performance of that duty while maintaining confidences of the client, however, is qualified by the advocate's duty of candor to the tribunal. Consequently, although a lawyer in an adversary proceeding is not required to present an impartial exposition of the law or to vouch for the evidence submitted in a cause, the lawyer must not allow the tribunal to be misled by false statements of law or fact or evidence that the lawyer knows to be false.

Representations by a Lawyer

[3]   An advocate is responsible for pleadings and other documents prepared for litigation, but is usually not required to have personal knowledge of matters asserted therein, for litigation documents ordinarily present asser-

tions by the client, or by someone on the client's behalf, and not assertions by the lawyer. Compare Rule 3.1. However, an assertion purporting to be on the lawyer's own knowledge, as in an affidavit by the lawyer or in a statement in open court, may properly be made only when the lawyer knows the assertion is true or believes it to be true on the basis of a reasonably diligent inquiry. There are circumstances where failure to make a disclosure is the equivalent of an affirmative misrepresentation. The obligation prescribed in Rule 1.2(d) not to counsel a client to commit or assist the client in committing a fraud applies in litigation. Regarding compliance with Rule 1.2(d), see the Comment to that Rule. See also the Comment to Rule 8.4(b).

Legal Argument

[4] Legal argument based on a knowingly false representation of law constitutes dishonesty toward the tribunal. A lawyer is not required to make a disinterested exposition of the law, but must recognize the existence of pertinent legal authorities. Furthermore, as stated in paragraph (a)(2), an advocate has a duty to disclose directly adverse authority in the controlling jurisdiction that has not been disclosed by the opposing party. The underlying concept is that legal argument is a discussion seeking to determine the legal premises properly applicable to the case.

Offering Evidence

[5] Paragraph (a)(3) requires that the lawyer refuse to offer evidence that the lawyer knows to be false, regardless of the client's wishes. This duty is premised on the lawyer's obligation as an officer of the court to prevent the trier of fact from being misled by false evidence. A lawyer does not violate this Rule if the lawyer offers the evidence for the purpose of establishing its falsity.

[6] If a lawyer knows that the client intends to testify falsely or wants the lawyer to introduce false evidence, the lawyer should seek to persuade the client that the evidence should not be offered. If the persuasion is ineffective and the lawyer continues to represent the client, the lawyer must refuse to offer the false evidence. If only a portion of a witness's testimony will be false, the lawyer may call the

witness to testify but may not elicit or otherwise permit the witness to present the testimony that the lawyer knows is false.

[7]   The duties stated in paragraphs (a) and (b) apply to all lawyers, including defense counsel in criminal cases. In some jurisdictions, however, courts have required counsel to present the accused as a witness or to give a narrative statement if the accused so desires, even if counsel knows that the testimony or statement will be false. The obligation of the advocate under the Rules of Professional Conduct is subordinate to such requirements. See also Comment [9].

[8]   The prohibition against offering false evidence only applies if the lawyer knows that the evidence is false. A lawyer's reasonable belief that evidence is false does not preclude its presentation to the trier of fact. A lawyer's knowledge that evidence is false, however, can be inferred from the circumstances. See Rule 1.0(f). Thus, although a lawyer should resolve doubts about the veracity of testimony or other evidence in favor of the client, the lawyer cannot ignore an obvious falsehood.

[9]   Although paragraph (a)(3) only prohibits a lawyer from offering evidence the lawyer knows to be false, it permits the lawyer to refuse to offer testimony or other proof that the lawyer reasonably believes is false. Offering such proof may reflect adversely on the lawyer's ability to discriminate in the quality of evidence and thus impair the lawyer's effectiveness as an advocate. Because of the special protections historically provided criminal defendants, however, this Rule does not permit a lawyer to refuse to offer the testimony of such a client where the lawyer reasonably believes but does not know that the testimony will be false. Unless the lawyer knows the testimony will be false, the lawyer must honor the client's decision to testify. See also Comment [7].

Remedial Measures

[10]   Having offered material evidence in the belief that it was true, a lawyer may subsequently come to know that the evidence is false. Or, a lawyer may be surprised when the lawyer's client, or another witness called by the lawyer, offers testimony the lawyer knows to be false, either during the lawyer's direct examination or in response to cross-

examination by the opposing lawyer. In such situations or if the lawyer knows of the falsity of testimony elicited from the client during a deposition, the lawyer must take reasonable remedial measures. In such situations, the advocate's proper course is to remonstrate with the client confidentially, advise the client of the lawyer's duty of candor to the tribunal and seek the client's cooperation with respect to the withdrawal or correction of the false statements or evidence. If that fails, the advocate must take further remedial action. If withdrawal from the representation is not permitted or will not undo the effect of the false evidence, the advocate must make such disclosure to the tribunal as is reasonably necessary to remedy the situation, even if doing so requires the lawyer to reveal information that otherwise would be protected by Rule 1.6. It is for the tribunal then to determine what should be done—making a statement about the matter to the trier of fact, ordering a mistrial or perhaps nothing.

[11] The disclosure of a client's false testimony can result in grave consequences to the client, including not only a sense of betrayal but also loss of the case and perhaps a prosecution for perjury. But the alternative is that the lawyer cooperate in deceiving the court, thereby subverting the truth-finding process which the adversary system is designed to implement. See Rule 1.2(d). Furthermore, unless it is clearly understood that the lawyer will act upon the duty to disclose the existence of false evidence, the client can simply reject the lawyer's advice to reveal the false evidence and insist that the lawyer keep silent. Thus the client could in effect coerce the lawyer into being a party to fraud on the court.

Preserving Integrity of Adjudicative Process

[12] Lawyers have a special obligation to protect a tribunal against criminal or fraudulent conduct that undermines the integrity of the adjudicative process, such as bribing, intimidating or otherwise unlawfully communicating with a witness, juror, court official or other participant in the proceeding, unlawfully destroying or concealing documents or other evidence or failing to disclose information to the tribunal when required by law to do so. Thus, paragraph (b) requires a lawyer to take reasonable remedial measures, including

disclosure if necessary, whenever the lawyer knows that a person, including the lawyer's client, intends to engage, is engaging or has engaged in criminal or fraudulent conduct related to the proceeding.

Duration of Obligation

[13]   A practical time limit on the obligation to rectify false evidence or false statements of law and fact has to be established. The conclusion of the proceeding is a reasonably definite point for the termination of the obligation. A proceeding has concluded within the meaning of this Rule when a final judgment in the proceeding has been affirmed on appeal or the time for review has passed.

Ex Parte Proceedings

[14]   Ordinarily, an advocate has the limited responsibility of presenting one side of the matters that a tribunal should consider in reaching a decision; the conflicting position is expected to be presented by the opposing party. However, in any ex parte proceeding, such as an application for a temporary restraining order, there is no balance of presentation by opposing advocates. The object of an ex parte proceeding is nevertheless to yield a substantially just result. The judge has an affirmative responsibility to accord the absent party just consideration. The lawyer for the represented party has the correlative duty to make disclosures of material facts known to the lawyer and that the lawyer reasonably believes are necessary to an informed decision.

Withdrawal

[15]   Normally, a lawyer's compliance with the duty of candor imposed by this Rule does not require that the lawyer withdraw from the representation of a client whose interests will be or have been adversely affected by the lawyer's disclosure. The lawyer may, however, be required by Rule 1.16(a) to seek permission of the tribunal to withdraw if the lawyer's compliance with this Rule's duty of candor results in such an extreme deterioration of the client-lawyer relationship that the lawyer can no longer competently represent the client. Also see Rule 1.16(b) for the circumstances in which a lawyer will be permitted to seek a tribunal's permission to withdraw. In connection with a

request for permission to withdraw that is premised on a client's misconduct, a lawyer may reveal information relating to the representation only to the extent reasonably necessary to comply with this Rule or as otherwise permitted by Rule 1.6.

RULE 3.4 FAIRNESS TO OPPOSING PARTY AND COUNSEL

A lawyer shall not:

(a) unlawfully obstruct another party' s access to evidence or unlawfully alter, destroy or conceal a document or other material having potential evidentiary value. A lawyer shall not counsel or assist another person to do any such act;

(b) falsify evidence, counsel or assist a witness to testify falsely, or offer an inducement to a witness that is prohibited by law;

(c) knowingly disobey an obligation under the rules of a tribunal except for an open refusal based on an assertion that no valid obligation exists;

(d) in pretrial procedure, make a frivolous discovery request or fail to make reasonably diligent effort to comply with a legally proper discovery request by an opposing party;

(e) in trial, allude to any matter that the lawyer does not reasonably believe is relevant or that will not be supported by admissible evidence, assert personal knowledge of facts in issue except when testifying as a witness, or state a personal opinion as to the justness of a cause, the credibility of a witness, the culpability of a civil litigant or the guilt or innocence of an accused; or

(f) request a person other than a client to refrain from voluntarily giving relevant information to another party unless:

(1) the person is a relative or an employee or other agent of a client; and

(2) the lawyer reasonably believes that the person's interests will not be adversely affected by refraining from giving such information.

Comment

[1] The procedure of the adversary system contemplates that the evidence in a case is to be marshalled competitively by the contending parties. Fair competition in the adversary system is secured by prohibitions against destruction or concealment of evidence, improperly influencing witnesses, obstructive tactics in discovery procedure, and the like.

[2] Documents and other items of evidence are often essential to establish a claim or defense. Subject to evidentiary privileges, the right of an opposing party, including the government, to obtain evidence through discovery or subpoena is an important procedural right. The exercise of that right can be frustrated if relevant material is altered, concealed or destroyed. Applicable law in many jurisdictions makes it an offense to destroy material for purpose of impairing its availability in a pending proceeding or one whose commencement can be foreseen. Falsifying evidence is also generally a criminal offense. Paragraph (a) applies to evidentiary material generally, including computerized information. Applicable law may permit a lawyer to take temporary possession of physical evidence of client crimes for the purpose of conducting a limited examination that will not alter or destroy material characteristics of the evidence. In such a case, applicable law may require the lawyer to turn the evidence over to the police or other prosecuting authority, depending on the circumstances.

[3] With regard to paragraph (b), it is not improper to pay a witness's expenses or to compensate an expert witness on terms permitted by law. The common law rule in most jurisdictions is that it is improper to pay an occurrence witness any fee for testifying and that it is improper to pay an expert witness a contingent fee.

[4] Paragraph (f) permits a lawyer to advise employees of a client to refrain from giving information to another party, for the employees may identify their interests with those of the client. See also Rule 4.2.

RULE 3.5 IMPARTIALITY AND DECORUM OF THE TRIBUNAL

A lawyer shall not:

(a) seek to influence a judge, juror, prospective juror or other official by means prohibited by law;

(b) communicate ex parte with such a person during the proceeding unless authorized to do so by law or court order;

(c) communicate with a juror or prospective juror after discharge of the jury if:

(1) the communication is prohibited by law or court order;

(2) the juror has made known to the lawyer a desire not to communicate; or

(3) the communication involves misrepresentation, coercion, duress or harassment; or

(d) engage in conduct intended to disrupt a tribunal.

Comment

[1] Many forms of improper influence upon a tribunal are proscribed by criminal law. Others are specified in the ABA Model Code of Judicial Conduct, with which an advocate should be familiar. A lawyer is required to avoid contributing to a violation of such provisions.

[2] During a proceeding a lawyer may not communicate ex parte with persons serving in an official capacity in the proceeding, such as judges, masters or jurors, unless authorized to do so by law or court order.

[3] A lawyer may on occasion want to communicate with a juror or prospective juror after the jury has been discharged. The lawyer may do so unless the communication is prohibited by law or a court order but must respect the desire of the juror not to talk with the lawyer. The lawyer may not engage in improper conduct during the communication.

[4] The advocate's function is to present evidence and argument so that the cause may be decided according to law. Refraining from abusive or obstreperous conduct is a corollary of the advocate's right to speak on behalf of litigants. A lawyer may stand firm against abuse by a judge but should avoid reciprocation; the judge's default is no justification for similar dereliction by an advocate. An advocate can present the cause, protect the record for subsequent review and

preserve professional integrity by patient firmness no less effectively than by belligerence or theatrics.

[5] The duty to refrain from disruptive conduct applies to any proceeding of a tribunal, including a deposition. See Rule 1.0(m).

RULE 3.6 TRIAL PUBLICITY

(a) A lawyer who is participating or has participated in the investigation or litigation of a matter shall not make an extrajudicial statement that the lawyer knows or reasonably should know will be disseminated by means of public communication and will have a substantial likelihood of materially prejudicing an adjudicative proceeding in the matter.

(b) Notwithstanding paragraph (a), a lawyer may state:

(1) the claim, offense or defense involved and, except when prohibited by law, the identity of the persons involved;

(2) information contained in a public record;

(3) that an investigation of a matter is in progress;

(4) the scheduling or result of any step in litigation;

(5) a request for assistance in obtaining evidence and information necessary thereto;

(6) a warning of danger concerning the behavior of a person involved, when there is reason to believe that there exists the likelihood of substantial harm to an individual or to the public interest; and

(7) in a criminal case, in addition to subparagraphs (1) through (6):

(i) the identity, residence, occupation and family status of the accused;

(ii) if the accused has not been apprehended, information necessary to aid in apprehension of that person;

(iii) the fact, time and place of arrest; and

(iv) the identity of investigating and arresting officers or agencies and the length of the investigation.

(c) Notwithstanding paragraph (a), a lawyer may make a statement that a reasonable lawyer would believe is required to protect a client from the substantial undue prejudicial effect of recent publicity not initiated by the lawyer or the lawyer's client. A statement made pursuant to this paragraph shall be limited to such information as is necessary to mitigate the recent adverse publicity.

(d) No lawyer associated in a firm or government agency with a lawyer subject to paragraph (a) shall make a statement prohibited by paragraph (a).

Comment

[1] It is difficult to strike a balance between protecting the right to a fair trial and safeguarding the right of free expression. Preserving the right to a fair trial necessarily entails some curtailment of the information that may be disseminated about a party prior to trial, particularly where trial by jury is involved. If there were no such limits, the result would be the practical nullification of the protective effect of the rules of forensic decorum and the exclusionary rules of evidence. On the other hand, there are vital social interests served by the free dissemination of information about events having legal consequences and about legal proceedings themselves. The public has a right to know about threats to its safety and measures aimed at assuring its security. It also has a legitimate interest in the conduct of judicial proceedings, particularly in matters of general public concern. Furthermore, the subject matter of legal proceedings is often of direct significance in debate and deliberation over questions of public policy.

[2] Special rules of confidentiality may validly govern proceedings in juvenile, domestic relations and mental disability proceedings, and perhaps other types of litigation. Rule 3.4(c) requires compliance with such rules.

[3] The Rule sets forth a basic general prohibition against a lawyer's making statements that the lawyer knows or should know will have a substantial likelihood of materially prejudicing an adjudicative proceeding. Recognizing that the public value of informed commentary is great and the likelihood of prejudice to a proceeding by the commentary of a lawyer

who is not involved in the proceeding is small, the rule applies only to lawyers who are, or who have been involved in the investigation or litigation of a case, and their associates.

[4] Paragraph (b) identifies specific matters about which a lawyer's statements would not ordinarily be considered to present a substantial likelihood of material prejudice, and should not in any event be considered prohibited by the general prohibition of paragraph (a). Paragraph (b) is not intended to be an exhaustive listing of the subjects upon which a lawyer may make a statement, but statements on other matters may be subject to paragraph (a).

[5] There are, on the other hand, certain subjects that are more likely than not to have a material prejudicial effect on a proceeding, particularly when they refer to a civil matter triable to a jury, a criminal matter, or any other proceeding that could result in incarceration. These subjects relate to:

(1) the character, credibility, reputation or criminal record of a party, suspect in a criminal investigation or witness, or the identity of a witness, or the expected testimony of a party or witness;

(2) in a criminal case or proceeding that could result in incarceration, the possibility of a plea of guilty to the offense or the existence or contents of any confession, admission, or statement given by a defendant or suspect or that person's refusal or failure to make a statement;

(3) the performance or results of any examination or test or the refusal or failure of a person to submit to an examination or test, or the identity or nature of physical evidence expected to be presented;

(4) any opinion as to the guilt or innocence of a defendant or suspect in a criminal case or proceeding that could result in incarceration;

(5) information that the lawyer knows or reasonably should know is likely to be inadmissible as evidence in a trial and that would, if disclosed, create a substantial risk of prejudicing an impartial trial; or

(6) the fact that a defendant has been charged with a crime, unless there is included therein a statement explaining that

the charge is merely an accusation and that the defendant is presumed innocent until and unless proven guilty.

[6]   Another relevant factor in determining prejudice is the nature of the proceeding involved. Criminal jury trials will be most sensitive to extrajudicial speech. Civil trials may be less sensitive. Non-jury hearings and arbitration proceedings may be even less affected. The Rule will still place limitations on prejudicial comments in these cases, but the likelihood of prejudice may be different depending on the type of proceeding.

[7]   Finally, extrajudicial statements that might otherwise raise a question under this Rule may be permissible when they are made in response to statements made publicly by another party, another party's lawyer, or third persons, where a reasonable lawyer would believe a public response is required in order to avoid prejudice to the lawyer's client. When prejudicial statements have been publicly made by others, responsive statements may have the salutary effect of lessening any resulting adverse impact on the adjudicative proceeding. Such responsive statements should be limited to contain only such information as is necessary to mitigate undue prejudice created by the statements made by others.

[8]   See Rule 3.8(f) for additional duties of prosecutors in connection with extrajudicial statements about criminal proceedings.

RULE 3.8 SPECIAL RESPONSIBILITIES OF A PROSECUTOR

The prosecutor in a criminal case shall:

(a) refrain from prosecuting a charge that the prosecutor knows is not supported by probable cause;

(b) make reasonable efforts to assure that the accused has been advised of the right to, and the procedure for obtaining, counsel and has been given reasonable opportunity to obtain counsel;

(c) not seek to obtain from an unrepresented accused a waiver of important pretrial rights, such as the right to a preliminary hearing;

(d) make timely disclosure to the defense of all evidence or information known to the prosecutor that tends to negate the guilt of the accused or mitigates

the offense, and, in connection with sentencing, disclose to the defense and to the tribunal all unprivileged mitigating information known to the prosecutor, except when the prosecutor is relieved of this responsibility by a protective order of the tribunal;

(e) not subpoena a lawyer in a grand jury or other criminal proceeding to present evidence about a past or present client unless the prosecutor reasonably believes:

(1) the information sought is not protected from disclosure by any applicable privilege;

(2) the evidence sought is essential to the successful completion of an ongoing investigation or prosecution; and

(3) there is no other feasible alternative to obtain the information;

(f) except for statements that are necessary to inform the public of the nature and extent of the prosecutor's action and that serve a legitimate law enforcement purpose, refrain from making extrajudicial comments that have a substantial likelihood of heightening public condemnation of the accused and exercise reasonable care to prevent investigators, law enforcement personnel, employees or other persons assisting or associated with the prosecutor in a criminal case from making an extrajudicial statement that the prosecutor would be prohibited from making under Rule 3.6 or this Rule.

Comment

[1] A prosecutor has the responsibility of a minister of justice and not simply that of an advocate. This responsibility carries with it specific obligations to see that the defendant is accorded procedural justice and that guilt is decided upon the basis of sufficient evidence. Precisely how far the prosecutor is required to go in this direction is a matter of debate and varies in different jurisdictions. Many jurisdictions have adopted the ABA Standards of Criminal Justice Relating to the Prosecution Function, which in turn are the product of prolonged and careful deliberation by lawyers experienced in both criminal prosecution and defense. Appli-

cable law may require other measures by the prosecutor and knowing disregard of those obligations or a systematic abuse of prosecutorial discretion could constitute a violation of Rule 8.4.

[2]   In some jurisdictions, a defendant may waive a preliminary hearing and thereby lose a valuable opportunity to challenge probable cause. Accordingly, prosecutors should not seek to obtain waivers of preliminary hearings or other important pretrial rights from unrepresented accused persons. Paragraph (c) does not apply, however, to an accused appearing *pro se* with the approval of the tribunal. Nor does it forbid the lawful questioning of an uncharged suspect who has knowingly waived the rights to counsel and silence.

[3]   The exception in paragraph (d) recognizes that a prosecutor may seek an appropriate protective order from the tribunal if disclosure of information to the defense could result in substantial harm to an individual or to the public interest.

[4]   Paragraph (e) is intended to limit the issuance of lawyer subpoenas in grand jury and other criminal proceedings to those situations in which there is a genuine need to intrude into the client-lawyer relationship.

[5]   Paragraph (f) supplements Rule 3.6, which prohibits extrajudicial statements that have a substantial likelihood of prejudicing an adjudicatory proceeding. In the context of a criminal prosecution, a prosecutor's extrajudicial statement can create the additional problem of increasing public condemnation of the accused. Although the announcement of an indictment, for example, will necessarily have severe consequences for the accused, a prosecutor can, and should, avoid comments which have no legitimate law enforcement purpose and have a substantial likelihood of increasing public opprobrium of the accused. Nothing in this Comment is intended to restrict the statements which a prosecutor may make which comply with Rule 3.6(b) or 3.6(c).

[6]   Like other lawyers, prosecutors are subject to Rules 5.1 and 5.3, which relate to responsibilities regarding lawyers and nonlawyers who work for or are associated with the lawyer's office. Paragraph (f) reminds the prosecutor of the importance of these obligations in connection with the

unique dangers of improper extrajudicial statements in a criminal case. In addition, paragraph (f) requires a prosecutor to exercise reasonable care to prevent persons assisting or associated with the prosecutor from making improper extrajudicial statements, even when such persons are not under the direct supervision of the prosecutor. Ordinarily, the reasonable care standard will be satisfied if the prosecutor issues the appropriate cautions to law-enforcement personnel and other relevant individuals.

RULE 4.2 COMMUNICATING WITH PERSON REPRESENTED BY COUNSEL

In representing a client, a lawyer shall not communicate about the subject of the representation with a person the lawyer knows to be represented by another lawyer in the matter, unless the lawyer has the consent of the other lawyer or is authorized to do so by law or a court order.

Comment

[1] This Rule contributes to the proper functioning of the legal system by protecting a person who has chosen to be represented by a lawyer in a matter against possible overreaching by other lawyers who are participating in the matter, interference by those lawyers with the client-lawyer relationship and the uncounselled disclosure of information relating to the representation.

[2] This Rule applies to communications with any person who is represented by counsel concerning the matter to which the communication relates.

[3] The Rule applies even though the represented person initiates or consents to the communication. A lawyer must immediately terminate communication with a person if, after commencing communication, the lawyer learns that the person is one with whom communication is not permitted by this Rule.

[4] This Rule does not prohibit communication with a represented person, or an employee or agent of such a person, concerning matters outside the representation. For example, the existence of a controversy between a government agency and a private party, or between two organiza-

tions, does not prohibit a lawyer for either from communicating with nonlawyer representatives of the other regarding a separate matter. Nor does this Rule preclude communication with a represented person who is seeking advice from a lawyer who is not otherwise representing a client in the matter. A lawyer may not make a communication prohibited by this Rule through the acts of another. See Rule 8.4(a). Parties to a matter may communicate directly with each other, and a lawyer is not prohibited from advising a client concerning a communication that the client is legally entitled to make. Also, a lawyer having independent justification or legal authorization for communicating with a represented person is permitted to do so.

[5]   Communications authorized by law may include communications by a lawyer on behalf of a client who is exercising a constitutional or other legal right to communicate with the government. Communications authorized by law may also include investigative activities of lawyers representing governmental entities, directly or through investigative agents, prior to the commencement of criminal or civil enforcement proceedings. When communicating with the accused in a criminal matter, a government lawyer must comply with this Rule in addition to honoring the constitutional rights of the accused. The fact that a communication does not violate a state or federal constitutional right is insufficient to establish that the communication is permissible under this Rule.

[6]   A lawyer who is uncertain whether a communication with a represented person is permissible may seek a court order. A lawyer may also seek a court order in exceptional circumstances to authorize a communication that would otherwise be prohibited by this Rule, for example, where communication with a person represented by counsel is necessary to avoid reasonably certain injury.

[7]   In the case of a represented organization, this Rule prohibits communications with a constituent of the organization who supervises, directs or regularly consults with the organization's lawyer concerning the matter or has authority to obligate the organization with respect to the matter or whose act or omission in connection with the matter may be imputed to the organization for purposes of civil or criminal

liability. Consent of the organization's lawyer is not required for communication with a former constituent. If a constituent of the organization is represented in the matter by his or her own counsel, the consent by that counsel to a communication will be sufficient for purposes of this Rule. Compare Rule 3.4(f). In communicating with a current or former constituent of an organization, a lawyer must not use methods of obtaining evidence that violate the legal rights of the organization. See Rule 4.4.

[8] The prohibition on communications with a represented person only applies in circumstances where the lawyer knows that the person is in fact represented in the matter to be discussed. This means that the lawyer has actual knowledge of the fact of the representation; but such actual knowledge may be inferred from the circumstances. See Rule 1.0(f). Thus, the lawyer cannot evade the requirement of obtaining the consent of counsel by closing eyes to the obvious.

[9] In the event the person with whom the lawyer communicates is not known to be represented by counsel in the matter, the lawyer's communications are subject to Rule 4.3.

RULE 4.3 DEALING WITH UNREPRESENTED PERSON

In dealing on behalf of a client with a person who is not represented by counsel, a lawyer shall not state or imply that the lawyer is disinterested. When the lawyer knows or reasonably should know that the unrepresented person misunderstands the lawyer's role in the matter, the lawyer shall make reasonable efforts to correct the misunderstanding. The lawyer shall not give legal advice to an unrepresented person, other than the advice to secure counsel, if the lawyer knows or reasonably should know that the interests of such a person are or have a reasonable possibility of being in conflict with the interests of the client.

Comment

[1] An unrepresented person, particularly one not experienced in dealing with legal matters, might assume that a lawyer is disinterested in loyalties or is a disinterested

authority on the law even when the lawyer represents a client. In order to avoid a misunderstanding, a lawyer will typically need to identify the lawyer's client and, where necessary, explain that the client has interests opposed to those of the unrepresented person. For misunderstandings that sometimes arise when a lawyer for an organization deals with an unrepresented constituent, see Rule 1.13(d).

[2] The Rule distinguishes between situations involving unrepresented persons whose interests may be adverse to those of the lawyer's client and those in which the person's interests are not in conflict with the client's. In the former situation, the possibility that the lawyer will compromise the unrepresented person's interests is so great that the Rule prohibits the giving of any advice, apart from the advice to obtain counsel. Whether a lawyer is giving impermissible advice may depend on the experience and sophistication of the unrepresented person, as well as the setting in which the behavior and comments occur. This Rule does not prohibit a lawyer from negotiating the terms of a transaction or settling a dispute with an unrepresented person. So long as the lawyer has explained that the lawyer represents an adverse party and is not representing the person, the lawyer may inform the person of the terms on which the lawyer's client will enter into an agreement or settle a matter, prepare documents that require the person's signature and explain the lawyer's own view of the meaning of the document or the lawyer's view of the underlying legal obligations.

RULE 8.4 MISCONDUCT

It is professional misconduct for a lawyer to:

(a) violate or attempt to violate the Rules of Professional Conduct, knowingly assist or induce another to do so, or do so through the acts of another;

(b) commit a criminal act that reflects adversely on the lawyer's honesty, trustworthiness or fitness as a lawyer in other respects;

(c) engage in conduct involving dishonesty, fraud, deceit or misrepresentation;

(d) engage in conduct that is prejudicial to the administration of justice;

(e) state or imply an ability to influence improperly a government agency or official or to achieve results by means that violate the Rules of Professional Conduct or other law; or

(f) knowingly assist a judge or judicial officer in conduct that is a violation of applicable rules of judicial conduct or other law.

Comment

[1]   Lawyers are subject to discipline when they violate or attempt to violate the Rules of Professional Conduct, knowingly assist or induce another to do so or do so through the acts of another, as when they request or instruct an agent to do so on the lawyer's behalf. Paragraph (a), however, does not prohibit a lawyer from advising a client concerning action the client is legally entitled to take.

[2]   Many kinds of illegal conduct reflect adversely on fitness to practice law, such as offenses involving fraud and the offense of willful failure to file an income tax return. However, some kinds of offenses carry no such implication. Traditionally, the distinction was drawn in terms of offenses involving "moral turpitude." That concept can be construed to include offenses concerning some matters of personal morality, such as adultery and comparable offenses, that have no specific connection to fitness for the practice of law. Although a lawyer is personally answerable to the entire criminal law, a lawyer should be professionally answerable only for offenses that indicate lack of those characteristics relevant to law practice. Offenses involving violence, dishonesty, breach of trust, or serious interference with the administration of justice are in that category. A pattern of repeated offenses, even ones of minor significance when considered separately, can indicate indifference to legal obligation.

[3]   A lawyer who, in the course of representing a client, knowingly manifests by words or conduct, bias or prejudice based upon race, sex, religion, national origin, disability, age, sexual orientation or socioeconomic status, violates paragraph (d) when such actions are prejudicial to the administration of justice. Legitimate advocacy respecting the foregoing factors does not violate paragraph (d). A trial judge's finding that peremptory challenges were exercised on a

discriminatory basis does not alone establish a violation of this rule.

[4]   A lawyer may refuse to comply with an obligation imposed by law upon a good faith belief that no valid obligation exists. The provisions of Rule 1.2(d) concerning a good faith challenge to the validity, scope, meaning or application of the law apply to challenges of legal regulation of the practice of law.

[5]   Lawyers holding public office assume legal responsibilities going beyond those of other citizens. A lawyer's abuse of public office can suggest an inability to fulfill the professional role of lawyers. The same is true of abuse of positions of private trust such as trustee, executor, administrator, guardian, agent and officer, director or manager of a corporation or other organization.

ABA STANDARDS FOR CRIMINAL JUSTICE: PROSECUTION FUNCTION (3RD ED. 1992)[1]

PART I.
GENERAL STANDARDS

Standard 3-1.1 The Function of the Standards

These standards are intended to be used as a guide to professional conduct and performance. They are not intended to be used as criteria for the judicial evaluation of alleged misconduct of the prosecutor to determine the validity of a conviction. They may or may not be relevant in such judicial evaluation, depending upon all the circumstances.

Standard 3-1.2 The Function of the Prosecutor

(a) The office of prosecutor is charged with responsibility for prosecutions in its jurisdiction.

(b) The prosecutor is an administrator of justice, an advocate, and an officer of the court; the prosecutor must exercise sound discretion in the performance of his or her functions.

(c) The duty of the prosecutor is to seek justice, not merely to convict.

(d) It is an important function of the prosecutor to seek to reform and improve the administration of criminal justice. When inadequacies or injustices in the substantive or proce-

---

1. Reprinted with the permission of the American Bar Association, 321 North Clark Street, Chicago, Illinois.

dural law come to the prosecutor's attention, he or she should stimulate efforts for remedial action.

(e) It is the duty of the prosecutor to know and be guided by the standards of professional conduct as defined by applicable professional traditions, ethical codes, and law in the prosecutor's jurisdiction. The prosecutor should make use of the guidance afforded by an advisory council of the kind described in standard 4–1.5.

Standard 3–1.3 Conflicts of Interest

(a) A prosecutor should avoid a conflict of interest with respect to his or her official duties.

(b) A prosecutor should not represent a defendant in criminal proceedings in a jurisdiction where he or she is also employed as a prosecutor.

(c) A prosecutor should not, except as law may otherwise expressly permit, participate in a matter in which he or she participated personally and substantially while in private practice or nongovernmental employment unless under applicable law no one is, or by lawful delegation may be, authorized to act in the prosecutor's stead in the matter.

(d) A prosecutor who has formerly represented a client in a matter in private practice should not thereafter use information obtained from that representation to the disadvantage of the former client unless the rules of attorney-client confidentiality do not apply or the information has become generally known.

(e) A prosecutor should not, except as law may otherwise expressly permit, negotiate for private employment with any person who is involved as an accused or as an attorney or agent for an accused in a matter in which the prosecutor is participating personally and substantially.

(f) A prosecutor should not permit his or her professional judgment or obligations to be affected by his or her own political, financial, business, property, or personal interests.

(g) A prosecutor who is related to another lawyer as parent, child, sibling, or spouse should not participate in the prosecution of a person who the prosecutor knows is represented by the other lawyer. Nor should a prosecutor who has a significant personal or financial relationship with another lawyer participate in the prosecution of a person who the prosecutor knows is represented by the other lawyer, unless the prosecutor's supervisor, if any, is informed and approves or unless there is no other prosecutor authorized to act in the prosecutor's stead.

(h) A prosecutor should not recommend the services of particular defense counsel to accused persons or witnesses unless requested by the accused person or witness to make such a recommendation, and should not make a referral that is likely to create a conflict of interest. Nor should a prosecutor comment upon the reputation or abilities of defense counsel to an accused person or witness who is seeking or may seek such counsel's services unless requested by such person.

Standard 3–1.4 Public Statements

(a) A prosecutor should not make or authorize the making of an extrajudicial statement that a reasonable person would expect to be disseminated by means of public communication if the prosecutor knows or reasonably should know that it will have a substantial likelihood of prejudicing a criminal proceeding.

(b) A prosecutor should exercise reasonable care to prevent investigators, law enforcement personnel, employees, or other persons assisting or associated with the prosecutor from making an extrajudicial statement that the prosecutor would be prohibited from making under this Standard.

Standard 3–1.5 Duty to Respond to Misconduct

(a) Where a prosecutor knows that another person associated with the prosecutor's office is engaged in action, intends to act or refuses to act in a manner that is a violation of a legal obligation to the prosecutor's office or a violation of law, the prosecutor should follow the policies of the prosecutor's office concerning such matters. If such policies are unavailing or do not exist, the prosecutor should ask the person to reconsider the action or inaction which is at issue if such a request is aptly timed to prevent such misconduct and is otherwise feasible. If such a request for reconsideration is unavailing, inapt or otherwise not feasible or if the seriousness of the matter so requires, the prosecutor should refer the matter to higher authority in the prosecutor's office, including, if warranted by the seriousness of the matter, referral to the chief prosecutor.

(b) If, despite the prosecutor's efforts in accordance with section (a), the chief prosecutor insists upon action, or a refusal to act, that is clearly a violation of law, the prosecutor may take further remedial action, including revealing the information necessary to remedy this violation to other appropriate government officials not in the prosecutor's office.

PART II.
ORGANIZATION OF THE PROSECUTION FUNCTION

Standard 3–2.1 Prosecution Authority to be Vested in a Public Official

The prosecution function should be performed by a public prosecutor who is a lawyer subject to the standards of professional conduct and discipline.

Standard 3–2.2 Interrelationship of Prosecution Offices Within a State

(a) Local authority and responsibility for prosecution is properly vested in a district, county, or city attorney. Wherever possible, a unit of prosecution should be designed on the basis of population, caseload, and other relevant factors sufficient to warrant at least one full-time prosecutor and the supporting staff necessary to effective prosecution.

(b) In some states, conditions such as geographical area and population may make it appropriate to create a statewide system of prosecution in which the state attorney general is the chief prosecutor and the local prosecutors are deputies.

(c) In all states, there should be coordination of the prosecution policies of local prosecution offices to improve the administration of justice and assure the maximum practicable uniformity in the enforcement of the criminal law throughout the state. A state association of prosecutors should be established in each state.

(d) To the extent needed, a central pool of supporting resources and personnel, including laboratories, investigators, accountants, special counsel, and other experts, should be maintained by the state government and should be available to assist all local prosecutors.

Standard 3–2.3 Assuring High Standards of Professional Skill

(a) The function of public prosecution requires highly developed professional skills. This objective can best be achieved by promoting continuity of service and broad experience in all phases of the prosecution function.

(b) Wherever feasible, the offices of chief prosecutor and staff should be full-time occupations.

(c) Professional competence should be the basis for selection for prosecutorial office. Prosecutors should select their personnel without regard to partisan political influence.

(d) Special efforts should be made to recruit qualified women and members of minority groups for prosecutorial office.

(e) In order to achieve the objective of professionalism and to encourage competent lawyers to accept such offices, compensation for prosecutors and their staffs should be commensurate with the high responsibilities of the office and comparable to the compensation of their peers in the private sector.

Standard 3–2.4 Special Assistants, Investigative Resources, Experts

(a) Funds should be provided to enable a prosecutor to appoint special assistants from among the trial bar experienced in criminal cases, as needed for the prosecution of a particular case or to assist generally.

(b) Funds should be provided to the prosecutor for the employment of a regular staff of professional investigative personnel and other necessary supporting personnel, under the prosecutor's direct control, to the extent warranted by the responsibilities and scope of the office; the prosecutor should also be provided with funds for the employment of qualified experts as needed for particular cases.

Standard 3–2.5 Prosecutor's Handbook; Policy Guidelines and Procedures

(a) Each prosecutor's office should develop a statement of (i) general policies to guide the exercise of prosecutorial discretion and (ii) procedures of the office. The objectives of these policies as to discretion and procedures should be to achieve a fair, efficient, and effective enforcement of the criminal law.

(b) In the interest of continuity and clarity, such statement of policies and procedures should be maintained in an office handbook. This handbook should be available to the public, except for subject matters declared "confidential," when it is reasonably believed that public access to their contents would adversely affect the prosecution function.

Standard 3–2.6 Training Programs

Training programs should be established within the prosecutor's office for new personnel and for continuing education of the staff. Continuing education programs for prosecutors should be substantially expanded and public funds should be provided to enable prosecutors to attend such programs.

Standard 3–2.7 Relations With Police

(a) The prosecutor should provide legal advice to the police concerning police functions and duties in criminal matters.

(b) The prosecutor should cooperate with police in providing the services of the prosecutor's staff to aid in training police in the performance of their function in accordance with law.

Standard 3–2.8 Relations With the Courts and Bar

(a) A prosecutor should not intentionally misrepresent matters of fact or law to the court.

(b) A prosecutor's duties necessarily involve frequent and regular official contacts with the judge or judges of the prosecutor's jurisdiction. In such contacts the prosecutor should carefully strive to preserve the appearance as well as the reality of the correct relationship which professional traditions, ethical codes, and applicable law require between advocates and judges.

(c) A prosecutor should not engage in unauthorized ex parte discussions with or submission of material to a judge relating to a particular case which is or may come before the judge.

(d) A prosecutor should not fail to disclose to the tribunal legal authority in the controlling jurisdiction known to the prosecutor to be directly adverse to the prosecutor's position and not disclosed by defense counsel.

(e) A prosecutor should strive to develop good working relationships with defense counsel in order to facilitate the resolution of ethical problems. In particular, a prosecutor should assure defense counsel that if counsel finds it necessary to deliver physical items which may be relevant to a pending case or investigation to the prosecutor, the prosecutor will not offer the fact of such delivery by defense counsel as evidence before a jury for purposes of establishing defense counsel's client's culpability. However, nothing in this Standard shall prevent a prosecutor from offering evidence of the fact of such delivery in a subsequent proceeding for the purpose of proving a crime or fraud in the delivery of the evidence.

Standard 3–2.9 Prompt Disposition of Criminal Charges

(a) A prosecutor should avoid unnecessary delay in the disposition of cases. A prosecutor should not fail to act with reasonable diligence and promptness in prosecuting an accused.

(b) A prosecutor should not intentionally use procedural devices for delay for which there is no legitimate basis.

(c) The prosecution function should be so organized and supported with staff and facilities as to enable it to dispose of all criminal charges promptly. The prosecutor should be punctual in attendance in court and in the submission of all motions, briefs, and other papers. The prosecutor should emphasize to all witnesses the importance of punctuality in attendance in court.

(d) A prosecutor should not intentionally misrepresent facts or otherwise mislead the court in order to obtain a continuance.

(e) A prosecutor, without attempting to get more funding for additional staff, should not carry a workload that, by reason of its excessive size, interferes with the rendering of quality representation, endangers the interests of justice in the speedy disposition of charges, or may lead to the breach of professional obligations.

Standard 3–2.10 Supercession and Substitution of Prosecutor

(a) Procedures should be established by appropriate legislation to the end that the governor or other elected state official is empowered by law to suspend and supersede a local prosecutor upon making a public finding, after reasonable notice and hearing, that the prosecutor is incapable of fulfilling the duties of office.

(b) The governor or other elected official should be empowered by law to substitute special counsel in the place of the local prosecutor in a particular case, or category of cases, upon making a public finding that this is required for the protection of the public interest.

Standard 3–2.11 Literary or Media Agreements

A prosecutor, prior to conclusion of all aspects of a matter, should not enter into any agreement or understanding by which the prosecutor acquires an interest in literary or media rights to a portrayal or account based in substantial part on information relating to that matter.

PART III.
INVESTIGATION FOR PROSECUTION DECISION

Standard 3–3.1 Investigative Function of Prosecutor

(a) A prosecutor ordinarily relies on police and other investigative agencies for investigation of alleged criminal acts, but the prosecutor has an affirmative responsibility to investigate suspected illegal activity when it is not adequately dealt with by other agencies.

(b) A prosecutor should not invidiously discriminate against or in favor of any person on the basis of race, religion, sex, sexual preference, or ethnicity in exercising discretion to investigate or to prosecute. A prosecutor should not use other improper considerations in exercising such discretion.

(c) A prosecutor should not knowingly use illegal means to obtain evidence or to employ or instruct or encourage others to use such means.

(d) A prosecutor should not discourage or obstruct communication between prospective witnesses and defense counsel. A prosecutor should not advise any person or cause any person to be advised to decline to give to the defense information which such person has the right to give.

(e) A prosecutor should not secure the attendance of persons for interviews by use of any communication which has the appearance or color of a subpoena or similar judicial process unless the prosecutor is authorized by law to do so.

(f) A prosecutor should not promise not to prosecute for prospective criminal activity, except where such activity is part of an officially supervised investigative and enforcement program.

(g) Unless a prosecutor is prepared to forgo impeachment of a witness by the prosecutor's own testimony as to what the witness stated in an interview or to seek leave to withdraw from the case in order to present the impeaching testimony, a prosecutor should avoid interviewing a prospective witness except in the presence of a third person.

Standard 3–3.2 Relations With Victims and Prospective Witnesses

(a) A prosecutor should not compensate a witness, other than an expert, for giving testimony, but it is not improper to reimburse an ordinary witness for the reasonable expenses of attendance upon court, attendance for depositions pursuant to statute or court rule, or attendance for pretrial interviews. Payments to a witness may be for transportation and loss of income, provided there is no attempt to conceal the fact of reimbursement.

(b) A prosecutor should advise a witness who is to be interviewed of his or her rights against self-incrimination and the right to counsel whenever the law so requires. It is also proper for a prosecutor to so advise a witness whenever the prosecutor knows or has reason to believe that the witness may be the subject of a criminal prosecution. However, a prosecutor should not so advise a witness for the purpose of influencing the witness in favor of or against testifying.

(c) The prosecutor should readily provide victims and witnesses who request it information about the status of cases in which they are interested.

(d) The prosecutor should seek to insure that victims and witnesses who may need protections against intimidation are advised of and afforded protections where feasible.

(e) The prosecutor should insure that victims and witnesses are given notice as soon as practicable of scheduling changes which will affect the victims' or witnesses' required attendance at judicial proceedings.

(f) The prosecutor should not require victims and witnesses to attend judicial proceedings unless their testimony is essential to the prosecution or is required by law. When their attendance is required, the prosecutor should seek to reduce to a minimum the time they must spend at the proceedings.

(g) The prosecutor should seek to insure that victims of serious crimes or their representatives are given timely notice of: (i) judicial proceedings relating to the victims' case; (ii) disposition of the case, including plea bargains, trial and sentencing; and (iii) any decision or action in the case which results in the accused's provisional or final release from custody.

(h) Where practical, the prosecutor should seek to insure that victims of serious crimes or their representatives are given an opportunity to consult with and to provide information to the prosecutor prior to the decision whether or not to prosecute, to pursue a disposition by plea, or to dismiss the charges.

Standard 3–3.3 Relations With Expert Witnesses

(a) A prosecutor who engages an expert for an opinion should respect the independence of the expert and should not seek to dictate the formation of the expert's opinion on the subject. To the extent necessary, the prosecutor should explain to the expert his or her role in the trial as an impartial expert called to aid the fact finders and the manner in which the examination of witnesses is conducted.

(b) A prosecutor should not pay an excessive fee for the purpose of influencing the expert's testimony or to fix the amount of the fee contingent upon the testimony the expert will give or the result in the case.

Standard 3–3.4 Decision to Charge

(a) The decision to institute criminal proceedings should be initially and primarily the responsibility of the prosecutor.

(b) Prosecutors should take reasonable care to ensure that investigators working at their direction or under their authority are adequately trained in the standards governing the issuance of arrest and search warrants and should inform investigators that they should seek the approval of a prosecutor in close or difficult cases.

(c) The prosecutor should establish standards and procedures for evaluating complaints to determine whether criminal proceedings should be instituted.

(d) Where the law permits a citizen to complain directly to a judicial officer or the grand jury, the citizen complainant should be required to present the complaint for prior approval to the prosecutor, and the prosecutor's action or recommendation thereon should be communicated to the judicial officer or grand jury.

Standard 3–3.5 Relations with Grand Jury

(a) Where the prosecutor is authorized to act as legal advisor to the grand jury, the prosecutor may appropriately explain the law and express an opinion on the legal significance of the evidence but should give due deference to its status as an independent legal body.

(b) The prosecutor should not make statements or arguments in an effort to influence grand jury action in a manner which would be impermissible at trial before a petit jury.

(c) The prosecutor's communications and presentations to the grand jury should be on the record.

Standard 3–3.6 Quality and Scope of Evidence Before Grand Jury

(a) A prosecutor should only make statements or arguments to the grand jury and only present evidence to the grand jury which the prosecutor believes is appropriate or authorized under law for presentation to the grand jury. In appropriate cases, the prosecutor may present witnesses to summarize admissible evidence available to the prosecutor which the prosecutor believes he or she will be able to present at trial. The prosecutor should also inform the grand jurors that they have the right to hear any available witnesses, including eyewitnesses.

(b) No prosecutor should knowingly fail to disclose to the grand jury evidence which tends to negate guilt or mitigate the offense.

(c) A prosecutor should recommend that the grand jury not indict if he or she believes the evidence presented does not warrant an indictment under governing law.

(d) If the prosecutor believes that a witness is a potential defendant, the prosecutor should not seek to compel the witness's testimony before the grand jury without informing the witness that he or she may be charged and that the witness should seek independent legal advice concerning his or her rights.

(e) The prosecutor should not compel the appearance of a witness before the grand jury whose activities are the subject of the inquiry if the witness states in advance that if called he or she will exercise the constitutional privilege not to testify, unless the prosecutor intends to judicially challenge the exercise of the privilege or to seek a grant of immunity according to the law.

(f) A prosecutor in presenting a case to a grand jury should not intentionally interfere with the independence of the grand jury, preempt a function of the grand jury, or abuse the processes of the grand jury.

(g) Unless the law of the jurisdiction so permits, a prosecutor should not use the grand jury in order to obtain tangible, documentary or testimonial evidence to assist the prosecutor in preparation for trial of a defendant who has already been charged by indictment or information.

(h) Unless the law of the jurisdiction so permits, a prosecutor should not use the grand jury for the purpose of aiding or assisting in any administrative inquiry.

Standard 3–3.7 Quality and Scope of Evidence for Information

Where the prosecutor is empowered to charge by information, the prosecutor's decisions should be governed by the principles embodied in Standards 3–3.6 and 3–3.9, where applicable.

Standard 3–3.8 Discretion as to Noncriminal Disposition

(a) The prosecutor should consider in appropriate cases the availability of noncriminal disposition, formal or informal, in deciding whether to press criminal charges which would otherwise be supported by probable cause; especially in the case of a first offender, the nature of the offense may warrant noncriminal disposition.

(b) Prosecutors should be familiar with the resources of social agencies which can assist in the evaluation of cases for diversion from the criminal process.

Standard 3–3.9 Discretion in the Charging Decision

(a) A prosecutor should not institute, or cause to be instituted, or permit the continued pendency of criminal charges when the prosecutor knows that the charges are not supported by probable cause. A prosecutor should not institute, cause to be instituted, or permit the continued pendency of criminal charges in the absence of sufficient admissible evidence to support a conviction.

(b) The prosecutor is not obliged to present all charges which the evidence might support. The prosecutor may in some circumstances and for good cause consistent with the public interest decline to prosecute, notwithstanding that sufficient evidence may exist which would support a conviction. Illustrative of the factors which the prosecutor may properly consider in exercising his or her discretion are:

    (i) the prosecutor's reasonable doubt that the accused is in fact guilty;

    (ii) the extent of the harm caused by the offense;

    (iii) the disproportion of the authorized punishment in relation to the particular offense or the offender;

    (iv) possible improper motives of a complainant;

    (v) reluctance of the victim to testify;

    (vi) cooperation of the accused in the apprehension or conviction of others; and

    (vii) availability and likelihood of prosecution by another jurisdiction.

(c) A prosecutor should not be compelled by his or her supervisor to prosecute a case in which he or she has a reasonable doubt about the guilt of the accused.

(d) In making the decision to prosecute, the prosecutor should give no weight to the personal or political advantages or disadvantages which might be involved or to a desire to enhance his or her record of convictions.

(e) In cases which involve a serious threat to the community, the prosecutor should not be deterred from prosecution by the fact that in the jurisdiction juries have tended to acquit persons accused of the particular kind of criminal act in question.

(f) The prosecutor should not bring or seek charges greater in number or degree than can reasonably be supported with evidence at trial or than are necessary to fairly reflect the gravity of the offense.

(g) The prosecutor should not condition a dismissal of charges, nolle prosequi, or similar action on the accused's relinquishment of the right to seek civil redress unless the accused has agreed to the action knowingly and intelligently, freely and voluntarily, and where such waiver is approved by the court.

Standard 3–3.10 Role in First Appearance and Preliminary Hearing

(a) A prosecutor who is present at the first appearance (however denominated) of the accused before a judicial officer should not communicate with the accused unless a waiver of counsel has been entered, except for the purpose of aiding in obtaining counsel or in arranging for the pretrial release of the accused. A prosecutor should not fail to make reasonable efforts to assure that the accused has been advised of the right to, and the procedure for obtaining, counsel and has been given reasonable opportunity to obtain counsel.

(b) The prosecutor should cooperate in good faith in arrangements for release under the prevailing system for pretrial release.

(c) The prosecutor should not seek to obtain from an unrepresented accused a waiver of important pretrial rights, such as the right to a preliminary hearing.

(d) The prosecutor should not seek a continuance solely for the purpose of mooting the preliminary hearing by securing an indictment.

(e) Except for good cause, the prosecutor should not seek delay in the preliminary hearing after an arrest has been made if the accused is in custody.

(f) The prosecutor should ordinarily be present at a preliminary hearing where such hearing is required by law.

Standard 3–3.11 Disclosure of Evidence by the Prosecutor

(a) A prosecutor should not intentionally fail to make timely disclosure to the defense, at the earliest feasible opportunity, of the existence of all evidence or information which tends to negate the guilt of the accused or mitigate the offense charged or which would tend to reduce the punishment of the accused.

(b) A prosecutor should not fail to make a reasonably diligent effort to comply with a legally proper discovery request.

(c) A prosecutor should not intentionally avoid pursuit of evidence because he or she believes it will damage the prosecution's case or aid the accused.

PART IV.
PLEA DISCUSSIONS

Standard 3–4.1 Availability for Plea Discussions

(a) The prosecutor should have and make known a general policy or willingness to consult with defense counsel concerning disposition of charges by plea.

(b) A prosecutor should not engage in plea discussions directly with an accused who is represented by defense counsel, except with defense counsel's approval. Where the defendant has properly waived counsel, the prosecuting attorney may engage in plea discussions with the defendant, although, where feasible, a record of such discussions should be made and preserved.

(c) A prosecutor should not knowingly make false statements or representations as to fact or law in the course of plea discussions with defense counsel or the accused.

Standard 3–4.2 Fulfillment of Plea Discussions

(a) A prosecutor should not make any promise or commitment assuring a defendant or defense counsel that a court will impose a specific sentence or a suspension of sentence; a prosecutor may properly advise the defense what position will be taken concerning disposition.

(b) A prosecutor should not imply a greater power to influence the disposition of a case than is actually possessed.

(c) A prosecutor should not fail to comply with a plea agreement, unless a defendant fails to comply with a plea agreement or other extenuating circumstances are present.

Standard 3–4.3 Record of Reasons for Nolle Prosequi Disposition

Whenever felony criminal charges are dismissed by way of nolle prosequi (or its equivalent), the prosecutor should make a record of the reasons for the action.

PART V.

THE TRIAL

Standard 3–5.1 Calendar Control

Control over the trial calendar should be vested in the court. The prosecuting attorney should advise the court of facts relevant in determining the order of cases on the court's calendar.

Standard 3–5.2 Courtroom Professionalism

(a) As an officer of the court, the prosecutor should support the authority of the court and the dignity of the trial courtroom by strict adherence to codes of professionalism and by manifesting a professional attitude toward the judge, opposing counsel, witnesses, defendants, jurors, and others in the courtroom.

(b) When court is in session, the prosecutor should address the court, not opposing counsel, on all matters relating to the case.

(c) A prosecutor should comply promptly with all orders and directives of the court, but the prosecutor has a duty to have the record reflect adverse rulings or judicial conduct which the prosecutor considers prejudicial. The prosecutor has a right to make respectful requests for reconsideration of adverse rulings.

(d) Prosecutors should cooperate with courts and the organized bar in developing codes of professionalism for each jurisdiction.

Standard 3–5.3 Selection of Jurors

(a) The prosecutor should prepare himself or herself prior to trial to discharge effectively the prosecution function in the selection of the jury and the exercise of challenges for cause and peremptory challenges.

(b) In those cases where it appears necessary to conduct a pretrial investigation of the background of jurors, investigatory methods of the prosecutor should neither harass nor unduly embarrass potential jurors or invade their privacy and, whenever possible, should be restricted to an investigation of records and sources of information already in existence.

(c) The opportunity to question jurors personally should be used solely to obtain information for the intelligent exercise of challenges. A prosecutor should not intentionally use the voir dire to present factual matter which the prosecutor knows will not be admissible at trial or to argue the prosecution's case to the jury.

Standard 3–5.4 Relations With Jury

(a) A prosecutor should not intentionally communicate privately with persons summoned for jury duty or impaneled as jurors prior to or during trial. The prosecutor should avoid the reality or appearance of any such communications.

(b) The prosecutor should treat jurors with deference and respect, avoiding the reality or appearance of currying favor by a show of undue solicitude for their comfort or convenience.

(c) After discharge of the jury from further consideration of a case, a prosecutor should not intentionally make comments to or ask questions of a juror for the purpose of harassing or embarrassing the juror in any way which will tend to influence judgment in future jury service. If the prosecutor believes that the verdict may be subject to legal challenge, he or she may properly, if no statute or rule prohibits such course, communicate with jurors to determine whether such challenge may be available.

Standard 3–5.5 Opening Statement

The prosecutor's opening statement should be confined to a statement of the issues in the case and the evidence the prosecutor intends to offer which the prosecutor believes in good faith will be available and admissible. A prosecutor should not allude to any evidence unless there is a good faith and reasonable basis for believing that such evidence will be tendered and admitted in evidence.

Standard 3–5.6 Presentation of Evidence

(a) A prosecutor should not knowingly offer false evidence, whether by documents, tangible evidence, or the testimony of witnesses, or fail to seek withdrawal thereof upon discovery of its falsity.

(b) A prosecutor should not knowingly and for the purpose of bringing inadmissible matter to the attention of the judge or jury offer inadmissible evidence, ask legally objectionable questions, or make other impermissible comments or arguments in the presence of the judge or jury.

(c) A prosecutor should not permit any tangible evidence to be displayed in the view of the judge or jury which would tend to prejudice fair consideration by the judge or jury until such time as a good faith tender of such evidence is made.

(d) A prosecutor should not tender tangible evidence in the view of the judge or jury if it would tend to prejudice fair consideration by the judge or jury unless there is a reasonable basis for its admission in evidence. When there is any substantial doubt about the admissibility of such evidence, it should be tendered by an offer of proof and a ruling obtained.

Standard 3–5.7 Examination of Witnesses

(a) The interrogation of all witnesses should be conducted fairly, objectively, and with due regard for the dignity and legitimate privacy of the witness, and without seeking to intimidate or humiliate the witness unnecessarily.

(b) The prosecutor's belief that the witness is telling the truth does not preclude cross-examination, but may affect the method and scope of cross-examination. A prosecutor should not use the power of cross-examination to discredit or undermine a witness if the prosecutor knows the witness is testifying truthfully.

(c) A prosecutor should not call a witness in the presence of the jury who the prosecutor knows will claim a valid privilege not to testify.

(d) A prosecutor should not ask a question which implies the existence of a factual predicate for which a good faith belief is lacking.

Standard 3–5.8 Argument to the Jury

(a) In closing argument to the jury, the prosecutor may argue all reasonable inferences from evidence in the record. The prosecutor should not intentionally misstate the evidence or mislead the jury as to the inferences it may draw.

(b) The prosecutor should not express his or her personal belief or opinion as to the truth or falsity of any testimony or evidence or the guilt of the defendant.

(c) The prosecutor should not make arguments calculated to appeal to the prejudices of the jury.

(d) The prosecutor should refrain from argument which would divert the jury from its duty to decide the case on the evidence.

Standard 3–5.9 Facts Outside the Record

The prosecutor should not intentionally refer to or argue on the basis of facts outside the record whether at trial or on appeal, unless such facts are matters of common public knowledge based on ordinary human experience or matters of which the court may take judicial notice.

Standard 3–5.10 Comments by Prosecutor After Verdict

The prosecutor should not make public comments critical of a verdict, whether rendered by judge or jury.

PART VI.

SENTENCING

Standard 3–6.1 Role in Sentencing

(a) The prosecutor should not make the severity of sentences the index of his or her effectiveness. To the extent that the prosecutor becomes involved in the sentencing process, he or she should seek to assure that a fair and informed judgment is made on the sentence and to avoid unfair sentence disparities.

(b) Where sentence is fixed by the court without jury participation, the prosecutor should be afforded the opportunity to address the court at sentencing and to offer a sentencing recommendation.

(c) Where sentence is fixed by the jury, the prosecutor should present evidence on the issue within the limits permitted in the jurisdiction, but the prosecutor should avoid introducing evidence bearing on sentence which will prejudice the jury's determination of the issue of guilt.

Standard 3–6.2 Information Relevant to Sentencing

(a) The prosecutor should assist the court in basing its sentence on complete and accurate information for use in the presentence report. The prosecutor should disclose to the court any information in the prosecutor's files relevant to the sentence. If incompleteness or inaccurateness in the presentence report comes to the prosecutor's attention, the prosecutor should take steps to present the complete and correct information to the court and to defense counsel.

(b) The prosecutor should disclose to the defense and to the court at or prior to the sentencing proceeding all unprivileged mitigating information known to the prosecutor, except when the prosecutor is relieved of this responsibility by a protective order of the tribunal.

*

Index

References are to Pages

171

†